PHOTO BY DARIO AYALA

Sir Ken Robinson, PhD, was an internationally recognized leader in the development of creativity, innovation, and human potential. For twelve years, he was professor of education at the University of Warwick in the UK. He also received honorary degrees from universities in the US and UK, as well as the Athena Award of the Rhode Island School of Design, the Peabody Medal for contributions to the arts and culture in the United States, the LEGO Prize for international achievement in education, the Benjamin Franklin Medal of the Royal Society of Arts, and the Nelson Mandela Changemaker Award. He advised governments, corporations, education systems, and some of the world's leading cultural organizations. His report, "All Our Futures: Creativity, Culture & Education" (The Robinson Report), has gained international critical acclaim. His prestigious TED Talk, "Do Schools Kill Creativity," is still to this day the most watched TED talk in history with over 80 million views and counting. It is estimated that it has been seen by 400 million viewers worldwide in 160 countries. He's a *New York Times* bestselling author, and his book, *The Element: How Finding Your Passion Changes Everything*, has been translated into twenty-three languages. In 2003 he received a knighthood from Queen Elizabeth II for his services to the arts. He died in 2020.

Kate Robinson is a writer, speaker, and co-founder of a number of initiatives dedicated to the legacy of her father, Sir Ken Robinson. These include the SKR Legacy Collective Fund, to celebrate and remember Sir Ken and continue his legacy through projects around the themes of education, environment, and culture; and Imagine if . . . , a nonprofit inspired by Sir Ken's passionate advocacy of human potential that culminates each year in a weeklong festival. She was the founding Editor in Chief and Head of Strategic Operations of HundrED, a Finnish initiative designed to seek and share the most inspiring innovations in education globally. She's also a patron of Action for Children's Arts and House of Imagination, as well as a board member at MindUp and codirector of Nevergrey; a company that works with organizations and individuals driven by social purpose. Her passion lies in engaging youth voice, and she was awarded a thought leadership award for Outstanding Contribution to Education Empowerment.

Also by Ken Robinson

You, Your Child, and School
Creative Schools
Finding Your Element
The Element
Out of Our Minds

Imagine If…

Creating a Future for Us All

Sir Ken Robinson, PhD,
and Kate Robinson

PENGUIN BOOKS

PENGUIN BOOKS
An imprint of Penguin Random House LLC
penguinrandomhouse.com

Illustrations by Alexis Seabrook

LIBRARY OF CONGRESS CATALOGING-IN-PUBLICATION DATA

Names: Robinson, Ken, 1950–2020, author. | Robinson, Kate (Consultant), author.
Title: Imagine if . . . : creating a future for us all /
Sir Ken Robinson and Kate Robinson.
Description: [New York, New York] : Penguin, [2022]
Identifiers: LCCN 2021038186 (print) | LCCN 2021038187 (ebook) |
ISBN 9780143134169 (paperback) | ISBN 9780525505907 (ebook)
Subjects: LCSH: Creative ability. | Creative thinking. | Educational change. |
Self-actualization (Psychology) | Self-realization.
Classification: LCC BF408 .R515499 2022 (print) | LCC BF408 (ebook) |
DDC 153.3/5—dc23/eng/20220114
LC record available at https://lccn.loc.gov/2021038186
LC ebook record available at https://lccn.loc.gov/2021038187

Printed in the United States of America
3rd Printing

Set in Leitura Roman 2 and Leitura Display
Designed by Sabrina Bowers

For Dad, my hero.
And for everyone he inspired.
—Kate Robinson

Acknowledgments

The core of this book has been in development for decades. It is, after all, an accumulation of a lifetime of work. My father's lifetime of work. It is even more significant, of course, because we had no idea when the proposal was being drafted or the agreements were being signed that he wouldn't be here to hold the finished book in his hands. That being said, there are two caveats to highlight before continuing.

The first is that there will no doubt be people whom Dad would have loved to acknowledge here, and who absolutely deserve the acknowledgment, but may be missing from the list. If you are one of these people, please know that it is absolutely not intentional, it is simply a result of not having Dad here to ask.

The second is that there are people who supported me and my family during the most difficult time we have known—losing Dad. These people gave their hearts to keep ours beating, even though they were breaking, and they deserve true acknowledgment and recognition. There are also people who contributed actively to Dad's work over the years, and they also deserve true acknowledgment and recognition. I'm afraid I haven't been able to include all these people here, for fear the pages of acknowledgments would outnumber the actual pages of the book itself. Dad lived an incredible life and had a monumental career—there is a place for a book dedicated to that alone, and should I write it I will include a more comprehensive list of acknowledgments than I have here. All that is to say, I have focused solely on the people who have helped in the process of making this particular book.

With those caveats out of the way, and all of us hopefully on the same page, here we go.

First and foremost, I must thank Dad. Not only for beginning this book, but for trusting me to finish it and for his confidence in me to do it justice. The same goes for the team at Penguin Viking for their patience, understanding, compassion, and support throughout this process: my first editor, Victoria Savanh for making the prospect of writing a book seem less terrifying, for bouncing ideas back and forth, and for elevating each draft with her spot-on feedback; then Gretchen Schmid, who took over when Victoria left Penguin and picked up the project seamlessly to guide me through the final stages of production and design to the book you are holding now. Josephine Greywoode at Penguin UK, who has shown kindness and consideration at every turn, and who has generously shared her expertise with me throughout. At Global Lion Management, my sincere thanks to Charlie Sarabian for being a true friend to Peter, for answering my hundreds of questions, and for always being there.

To Sophie Britton, our incredible EA, a published author in her own right, who read every single draft before I was brave enough to send it to Penguin, and whose feedback and advice have been an invaluable lifeline. I also must thank Sophie, although I may be the only one, for closing my diary entirely while I was writing and patiently rescheduling every meeting I snuck in and then inevitably realized I couldn't make.

There are two people who deserve outstanding mention, for keeping me sane, hydrated, and fed. They read every single draft, edit, and rewrite, and kept me moving forward when I didn't feel capable of it: my beautiful mum, Therese, was a north star representing Dad at every turn. Having worked with Dad for forty-four years, she was as close to having him in the room as is possible, and despite her own grief she showed up to help me day after day after day; and my husband, Anthony, who has been my rock during these past several months. He made endless cups of tea, walked with me for hours when I was faced with writer's block or a difficult concept, and all while keeping the other areas of our business thriving. He never once complained when I was absentminded, or too tired to talk, and when I had nothing else to give, he gave his everything to our daughter, so she never noticed.

To our daughter, Adeline, who had just turned three when I disappeared to write, and my stepson, Charlie, thank you both from the bottom of my heart for all of the laughter and love you gave throughout.

And thank you to Janet and Robin, my in-laws, for keeping both kids entertained and full of "Granddad Cake" on all the days I was up against a deadline.

There are people who have given an abundance of time, energy, advice, and support in the creation of the book, and I am forever grateful to each of them: Amir Amedi, Kanya Balakrishna, Graham Barkus, Jeff Bezos, China Bialos, Heston Blumenthal, Damian Bradfield, Zoe Camp, Alexa Collis, Jackie

Cooper, May Delaney, Ted Dinersmith, Julie Epstein, Helen Hatzis, Goldie Hawn, Drew Herdener, Ken Hertz, Michael Hynes, Rami Kleinmann, Megan Leigh, Lasse Leponiemi, Andrew Mangino, George Monbiot, Jon Polk, James Robinson, Pasi Sahlberg, Tim Smit, Simon Taffler, Rachel Womack, and our amazing Patreon community.

In Loving Memory of Peter Miller
1948–2021

Peter Miller, the Literary Lion, was Dad's literary agent for fifteen years. He oversaw the creation of *The Element*, *Finding Your Element*, *Creative Schools*, *You, Your Child, and School*, every new edition of *Out of Our Minds*, and finally *Imagine If . . .* He sold the books all around the world and into thirty countries. He was passionate about his work and about his clients. When Dad passed away, he transferred this passion and commitment over to me. Peter became one of my biggest champions, and it is no exaggeration to say that I would not have been able to write this without him in my corner. In fact, this book was originally his idea—a short manifesto of Dad's core beliefs was his vision. It feels impossible to believe that he is not here to see it published, but I take great comfort that he read the final manuscript and that he knew the book was at last becoming a reality. Peter was more than our agent; he was a part of our family. I feel lucky to have known him, and to have benefited from his wisdom and expertise while writing this book. His legacy lives on in the lives that he touched and in the collection of books that only exist because he believed in their authors.

Contents

Our creative powers have brought untold benefits to the comforts of our lives, the health of our bodies, and the complexity of our cultures. They have also brought us to a critical pass.

1 The Human Advantage   1

Imagination is what separates us from the rest of life on Earth. It is through imagination that we create the worlds in which we live. We can also re-create them.

Foreword

There is a famous quote attributed to the French philosopher and mathematician Blaise Pascal: "I would have written a shorter letter, but I did not have the time." It is also attributed, in various forms, to Mark Twain, Winston Churchill, John Locke, Woodrow Wilson, and Benjamin Franklin, among others. I'm sure they all said versions of the same thing, and having now finished this book, I fully understand what they meant. There's nothing quite so time-consuming as trying to be brief.

The book you are holding is purposefully concise, but within its pages is a lifetime of work. Not just any lifetime, but the lifetime of a man who inspired, encouraged, and championed millions. A man who assured people all around the world that it wasn't them or their loved ones who were broken, but the system. A man I was lucky enough to call my father.

Dad was incredibly gifted, but he was also a gift himself. He was a rare mix of articulate, sharp, funny, humble, and kind. He was present in every conversation he had, regardless of who it was with, and in a world where people are constantly distracted or looking over their shoulder to see who else might walk in, that stood out. He made everyone he met feel special because he had a knack for seeing what was special in everyone he met. Being around him, you knew that you were in the company of someone extraordinary, but in truth, it is only now that he is gone that I understand just how rare he was. I will spend the rest of my life coming to terms with the fact that he is gone, but I will also spend it dedicated to the fact that his work lives on. In fact, the world has never needed his message more.

At its core, Dad's work was a love letter to human potential. It was, of course, a deep criticism of many of the systems that we have come to take for granted, and it was an uncompromising exposé of their many failings. But ultimately, it was a declaration that we are capable of more. That each and every one of us is a fountain of talent and resources, and if we were to dedicate our efforts to nurturing this potential rather than systematically suppressing it, the world would be a much better place for us all.

Dad dedicated his life to this vision. He started writing the book you are holding in 2017, but this book began a very long time before that. I'm sure he would make the case that it began before he was even born. He was the first to say that the arguments he made were not new—they have deep roots in the history of teaching and learning since ancient times. They are based on principles that have always inspired humanity, but that we have drastically lost sight of. As such, he stood in a long tradition, and it is my honor to stand alongside him.

I was privileged to work with Dad for a number of years, and when we received his prognosis in the summer of 2020, I made him a promise: I would dedicate my life to continuing his work. We spent much of his final days talking about what that would entail and working together on this book.

I will hold the memory of those days in my heart forever.

It was clear then that embarking on this project would be a combination of finding comfort in his words and message, and agony in not being able to ask him what he meant or throw an idea around together. This has been an experience unlike any other. Nothing could have prepared me for the journey of these past several months, for losing him and for trying to make sense of the world without him in it. But through it all—the doubts, the questions, the inspiration, the grief—there has been one simple guiding light: He believed that I could do it. He believed that we all could.

This book began as an abridgment of his wider work. It is now so much more than that—it is the entrustment of a life's mission. It is a rallying cry for the millions of people he inspired, and the millions more he will inspire, to continue to fight for the changes we urgently need. The revolution is well under way. It requires us to see the potential in each of us individually, and all of us collectively, the way Dad did.

Imagine if we used our incredible capacities to create a world in which every person had a deep understanding of their own unique talents. Imagine if we built systems that lifted us up instead of keeping us down. Imagine if we embraced our diversities rather than running from them. We have come to a point in our history in which continuing to do what we have always done is no longer an option. We must do better. It begins, as it always does, with each of us taking a stand.

Imagine if . . .

Kate Robinson
WINDSOR, JUNE 2021

Preface

How should we educate our children? For generations we have been getting this badly wrong. It is more urgent than ever to get it right. The world is undergoing revolutionary changes. To meet them we need a revolution in education.

I've been around education for more than fifty years. A lot of things have changed in that time—and a lot of things have not. For most of my professional life I've been pushing for fundamental changes in education to give more people a better chance of leading the lives they deserve. Children are born with boundless capacities: what becomes of them has everything to do with how they are educated. Education has two main roles in people's lives: it should help them to develop their natural capacities and to make their way in the world around them. Too often, it falls tragically short on both counts.

I have written, talked, and agitated about all of this for a long time. I've been involved in numerous initiatives around the world, written a raft of publications, and given thousands of presentations. I'm often asked: What, if I were to boil it all down, are the specific changes I'm pushing for, and why? Boiling it down is what I've tried to do here. This is my distilled view of the challenges we face, the changes that are needed, and the practical steps we can take.

There are three main themes. First, we are living in times of revolution and face unprecedented challenges—as individuals, as communities, and as a species. These challenges are largely of our own making. That means we can do something about them. Second, if we're to do that, we have to think differently about our children and ourselves. Third, we have to do things differently in education, at work, and in our communities.

If you've read my other books, you'll recognize some of the arguments and language in this one. This is a distillation, after all. If you haven't read them, I hope you will. They offer a lot of evidence and practical examples. If you don't have the time, this is the bottom line. I hope you find it thought-provoking and useful. The issues could hardly be more important.

Ken Robinson
LOS ANGELES, OCTOBER 2019

Introduction

Our creative powers have brought untold benefits to the comforts of our lives, the health of our bodies, and the complexity of our cultures. They have also brought us to a critical pass.

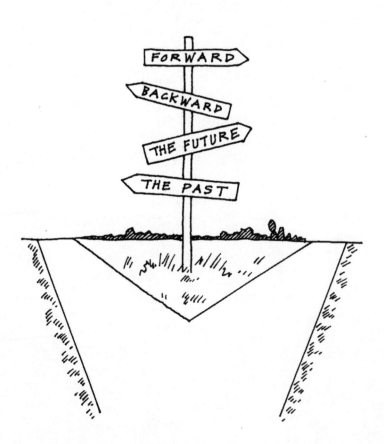

Here you are. Today may be a day like any other day, or it might feel somehow different. Perhaps you are in a situation that is familiar to you, or maybe you're somewhere brand new doing something you've never done before. In any case, here you are: a living, breathing part of this world that we all share.

Whatever your situation, the environment around you and the things you can see, smell, and touch are different from those experienced by the generations who came before you. Even if you were to be sitting in a home that has belonged to your family for hundreds of years—the circumstances around you would be unrecognizable to your predecessors. Your earliest ancestors would have been incapable of comprehending the concept of a book, let alone reading one. Their descendants would have been blown away by the idea of mass production and publishing. Their children and their children's children, all the way down to your great-grandparents, would be shaken to their core by the concept of an e-reader, laptop, or smartphone. You get the point: for all of human history the world has developed, evolved, and advanced. It continues to do so at an ever-quickening rate, and we are the reason why.

In the coming pages, we will look at what makes human

beings just so special in comparison to other creatures on Earth. We will highlight some of the reasons the world around you looks the way it does, and how it came to be. And we will discuss how many of the systems of which we are all a part are no longer fit for purpose. Education is one such system.

Education has the potential to radically change the course of a child's life for the better. This is true of all children from all sorts of backgrounds. But it doesn't happen automatically, and it doesn't happen often enough. The teaching profession is full of wonderful, dedicated individuals who are passionate about the work they do, but who are too often undervalued. They work within a system that inhibits the freedom they require to make autonomous decisions and truly create the positive impact they are capable of. The effect of education on a person's life depends on the sort of school they go to and the teachers they have. Too often, education demoralizes young people rather than bolsters them, and denies them the very opportunities they need to succeed in their lives. The reasons have to do with how current systems of education have evolved.

For generations, education has been biased toward narrow forms of academic ability, and as such it disregards the marvelous diversity of young people's talents and interests. On top of that, governments around the world have been spending fortunes on "reforming" education to "raise standards." These efforts have mostly been an appalling waste of energy, time, and money. They are based on wrongheaded assumptions about children and learning and the world we are actually living in. They have marginalized the very capabilities our children need to create a more equitable and sustainable world, including creativity, critical thinking, citizenship, collaboration, and compassion.

As we face an increasingly febrile future, the answer is not to do better what we've done before. We have to do something else. We have to take stock of the position we are all in and radically rethink how we move forward. We must urgently reimagine education and schools. Life has always been turbulent. Even so and by any measure, the challenges we face now are of a different order. Education is not the sole cause of these crises, but it is thoroughly implicated in them. In 1934 the psychologist Jean Piaget said, "Only education is capable of saving our societies from possible collapse, whether violent or gradual," History provides many examples. The visionary novelist H. G. Wells put the point even more sharply: "Human history," he said, "is a race between education and catastrophe." The evidence suggests that he and Piaget were right.

You may have noticed that this is a short book. I think of it more as a long letter. The nature of a short book, or a long letter, is that we will cover a lot of things in a small amount of time. If you are familiar with my work, you may recognize some of the arguments in the coming pages. If you are not familiar and have questions about something you read here, I suggest you have a look at my other books, as they explore a lot of the topics more deeply and give tangible examples from all around the world of the changes we are arguing for.

What you are about to read is an urgent plea that we stop,

take stock, and correct the course we are on. Our actions have led us to a tipping point of doing more harm than good. We are systematically stripping the Earth of its natural resources, and ourselves of our human resources. If we continue to behave as we are, we will deprive ourselves and our children of a healthy planet to call home as well as the skills we will all need to develop if we are to have a future at all. The good news is that the solutions are well within our power. The stakes could not be higher, but we have everything we need to get it right.

1

The Human Advantage

Imagination is what separates us from the rest of life on Earth. It is through imagination that we create the worlds in which we live. We can also re-create them.

In many respects, we humans are like most of the rest of life on Earth. We are made of flesh and blood, and ultimately our lives depend on what the Earth provides. If all goes well, we grow from tiny seeds, through infancy and maturity, to old age, and ultimately we die. Like all living things, we rely on the bounty of the Earth to live at all, and we survive and flourish in certain conditions and wither and fade in others. There is one way, however, in which we are remarkably different from the rest of life around us, and that is our unique powers of imagination. It is because of our ability to imagine that we don't live in the world as other creatures do, we create the worlds in which we live.

This is not to say that no other creature on Earth is capable of imagination or has any form of imaginative ability, but certainly none comes close to showing the complex abilities of imagination that humans have. While other creatures communicate in their own distinct ways, none comes close to the virtuosity of human speech. Some may sing and dance, but they don't perform spoken-word poetry or multi-act ballets, or coordinate flash mobs. They may gaze at the night sky, but they don't estimate the negative energy of black holes or build miraculous craft to travel in space. We do. So far as we know, we are the most inventive creatures ever to walk the Earth. In cosmic time, our lives are as brief as the beat of a wing. Yet we are endowed with immense powers of imagination, through which we can transcend the limits of space and time.

Imagination is the ability to bring to mind things that are not immediately present to our senses. With our imaginations we can step out of the here and now: we can speculate, visualize, and suppose. We can revisit the past, anticipate the future, see as others see, and feel as others feel. Imagination is multifaceted. It includes the ability to have mental experiences that can be described as *imaginal*—bringing to mind images drawn from real experiences, for example, your mother's hair or what you ate for lunch yesterday; *imaginative*—bringing to mind images of things you have never experienced, such as a green dog on roller skates, or a vision of how you might spend your next vacation; and *imaginary*—confusing imaginative experiences with real ones, like in a vivid dream or hallucination. Because our imagination allows us to envision the future, it is an essential part of being able to shape and build it.

Applied Imagination

You could be imaginative all day long without doing anything about it, and as such, nothing would ever change. To make use of our imaginations we need to take them one step further: we need to be creative. If imagination is the ability to bring to mind things that are not present to our senses, then creativity is the process of putting your imagination to work. It is applied imagination. Imagination allows us to envision alternative possibilities, and creativity equips us with the tools to bring them into existence.

I define creativity as the process of having original ideas that have value. This definition is based on the work of the All Our Futures group, and it includes three key terms to note: *process*, *originality*, and *value*.

1. Creativity is a *process*, which means it includes a relationship between two main aspects that bounce off each other: generating ideas and evaluating ideas. Creative pursuits involve swapping back and forth between the two: generating a new idea, trialing it, evaluating it, using this evaluation to generate an alternative new idea, or amendment to the original idea, trialing this new version, evaluation, and on and on. While possible, it is rare that a final product—be it a piece of art, a scientific discovery, or a recipe—is conceived in its finished form. More often than not, ideas come half-baked and are chiseled and tweaked, scrapped and thrown away, then resurrected in new forms, before the best outcome is discovered. This is true of even the most renowned: it is believed that it took Leonardo da Vinci four years to complete the *Mona Lisa*; and when describing her writing process, Maya Angelou famously stated, "It takes me forever to get it to sing. I *work* at the language." Ideas in this process are vulnerable. An idea with potential may be

damaged beyond repair if criticized or dismissed too early. Misunderstanding the process is why many people become disillusioned and think they are not creative.

2. Creativity involves *originality*. There are different ways to categorize originality in this context, and each is valid: if it is original in relation to the creator's previous work; if it is original in relation to the work of the creator's contemporaries; or if it is original in relation to all of history, if a piece of work is the first of its kind to ever be created.

3. Creativity involves making judgments of *value*. What is considered to be of value depends on the nature and the purpose of the work—if something is useful, beautiful, valid, or sustainable, etc. For example, beauty is one aspect of value to aim for when designing a building, but it soon becomes irrelevant if the structure of the building is unsound. For an original design of a building to have value it must be both aesthetically pleasing and be fit for purpose. In this sense, and across all three points, the creative process depends heavily on the ability to think critically.

The capacity for creativity is inherent in all of us. Imagination and creativity are at the heart of all uniquely human achievements, and those achievements have been dazzling. Look around—we have generated numerous languages, elegant systems of mathematics, revelatory sciences, revolutionary technologies, intricate economies, soul-searching art forms, and a vast diversity of cultural beliefs and practices.

Call and Response

There is a myth that we often hold to be true: that our lives are linear. This myth tells us that we are born, we grow, we go to school, and if we work hard and pass the tests, we graduate and go on to university. In university, if we work hard, we will earn a degree and go on to employment. Once employed, if we work hard, we will work our way up the ladder of success. One day we will retire and live out our days worry-free, basking in the glow of a life well lived. While it's a pretty story, it is for the most part fictional. Life may work like this for a small group of people. And yes, we may all begin as babies and grow at roughly the same rate as one another, and there may be various milestones we all aim to hit at certain points along the way, but the actual flow of our lives is much more fluid than this story would have us believe. For most of us, the only time our lives look this sequential and intentional is when we sit down to write our résumés, at which point we do our absolute best to hide the total chaos we've been living through in order to make it seem like we've been following an elaborate life plan.

The story doesn't account for the highs and lows, the bumps and twists, the dead ends and backtracks, the starting again in new directions, the falling down and getting back up. It doesn't account for the unexpected opportunities, the impulse decisions, the learning and development, the situations out of our control, and the growth that comes from all of this. Life is rarely a straight line moving upward across a page. Real life is more like a beautiful scribble, looping across the page. Life is complex and unpredictable, and because of our powers of imagination and creativity we are able to navigate it.

It is because of the billions of scribbles that have interwoven across humanity's time on Earth that our world looks the way it does now. As a species we have continually created new tools and technologies to enhance our experience—be it the axe, the fishing rod, the wheel, the car, or the smartphone. One of our strongest assets is our ability to build upon the work of others, to be collaborative. When Tim Berners-Lee invented the World Wide Web, he began by standing on the shoulders of the giants who came before him, making use of the thoughts and developments of his peers and predecessors. His primary goal was to help academics share their work. He could not have anticipated the ways in which his invention would change almost every aspect of life as we know it. His technology lit a spark in the minds of others who took it and ran with it. His invention laid the foundations for others to build upon—from the serial entrepreneur running multibillion-dollar businesses, to the seven-year-old building worlds from scratch in *Minecraft*, to the home crafter finding a market for her creations.

Breakthrough technologies always have unintended consequences. When Gutenberg perfected his printing press in 1450, he didn't expect it to foment the Protestant Reformation a century later. His aim was to start a profitable small business. When Sir Michael Faraday explored the physics of electricity in the 1820s, he didn't anticipate nuclear power stations or death metal.

The pioneers of the automobile didn't anticipate fracking or global warming. When Steve Jobs and the team were getting the bugs out of the iPhone in 2006, they didn't foresee the millions of apps or the mixed blessings of social media. How could they? That's not how creativity and culture work. Creativity is call and response: one idea can catalyze a multitude more in the minds of other people.

A Critical Pass

In many respects we are physically evolving at the same rate as other animals; culturally we are evolving exponentially, and in ways that no other species has shown capacity for. The rate of change in our societies and cultures today is unprecedented—in less than a generation our ways of life have become almost unrecognizable. We are more connected than any generation before us, we have access to information at our very fingertips, our lives are almost becoming as virtual as they are physical. We do not exist in the world as we find it, our lives are not limited to the locations or climates we are born into. We form ideas about the world around us and are therefore able to adapt it to better suit our interests. Over the centuries of human life, we have shaped and reshaped our existences. In doing so, we have reached a critical point in our evolution. It is time to take stock of what kind of a world we have created, and what it means to be human in it.

2

The World We Have Created

The human world is shaped by the ideas, beliefs, and values of human imagination and culture. It is created out of our minds as much as from the natural environment.

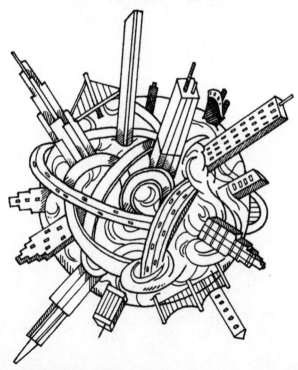

Earth's position in the universe is small and relatively insignificant. It is dwarfed by its neighboring planets Jupiter, Saturn, Uranus, and Neptune, the size of a grape seed compared to the Sun, and just one of an infinite number of twinkles from a cosmic perspective. Yet as Carl Sagan so eloquently put it: "On it, everyone you love, everyone you know, everyone you ever heard of, every human being who ever was, lived out their lives."

We're still searching for evidence of life on other planets. As far as we can tell, the majority of the ones we can reach orbit lifelessly in space. But our planet is teeming with life. One of the miracles of the natural world is the sheer variety of it: its ecosystems, species, and climates. The same is true of the human world, with its breathtaking diversity of cultures, belief systems, and traditions. Our world is not only shaped by its position relative to the Sun, the existence of water, and the topography of the continents, but also by the ideas, beliefs, and values of human imagination and culture.

The majority of the world that you and I recognize today is the result of human activity over centuries. The location of our cities, the ways in which our businesses and structures are run, how our education systems are designed, our modes of transport, and the law and order we are obliged to keep have all been carefully and strategically crafted by us. By that, I don't mean you and me specifically, but by other humans who came before us. While we inhabit a natural world, we exist in a devised one. Every generation lives through its own unique set of circumstances, and in doing so leaves indelible marks for future generations to make sense of. The unique set of circumstances we find ourselves navigating are in part born from the crosscurrents of three global forces: demography, technology, and ideology.

Demography

Human beings emerged as a species roughly between 150,000 and 200,000 years ago. Over the course of the time since, it is estimated that 100 billion people like you and me have lived and died on Earth. That's about 10,000 generations of humanity, of which we are the latest, and arguably the most attractive and well groomed.

For most of human history, however, populations were small, scattered, and slow to grow. Peckish predators, nimble prey, and harsh living conditions meant that life for most of our ancestors was a rather brief and unpleasant affair. In Europe that only began to change about 300 years, or fifteen generations, ago in the eighteenth century. The revolutionary period we now call the Enlightenment brought an enormous shift in human thought, first in Europe and eventually around most of the rest of the world. Challenging age-old dogma, philosophers and scientists argued that to understand the world around us, and our place within it, it was essential to elevate reason over superstition and evidence over belief. The cascade of discoveries and inventions that burst forth would eventually lead to the first Industrial Revolution, which in turn created unprecedented innovations in energy, manufacturing, transport, agriculture, hygiene, and medicine.

As conditions improved, populations grew rapidly. In 1800 the world population was 1 billion. In 1930 it was 2 billion. By 1960 it was 3 billion; it's now 7.7 billion, and we're heading for 10 billion by the middle of the century and over 11 billion by the end of it. We are by far the largest population of human beings ever to inhabit the Earth at the same time. Almost 10 percent of the 100 billion people who have ever lived are here right now.

Technology

Our lives have always been shaped by the tools we use. Tools extend our physical abilities; a wrench, a telescope, a printer enables us to do things that would otherwise be impossible. They also extend our minds and enable us to think things that might otherwise be inconceivable. From the plow to electricity, ingenious technologies have reconfigured whole civilizations. When

Galileo looked through a telescope in the fifteenth century, he saw the planets up close and personal for the first time. That new perspective led him to reconceive our place in the cosmos, and ultimately upend everything that had previously been taken for granted.

In our own times and in less than a generation, digital technologies have led us to remodel virtually every aspect of how we work and play, of how we relate to each other and how we don't.[1] People everywhere use them for everything, from checking facts to picking partners and booking holidays. Go to any public space and almost everyone is peering solipsistically into small screens at the gathering clouds of information that are always just a click away. The digital revolution has hardly begun. We are still understanding and navigating these new technologies and just what they mean—for each of us individually as well as for our societies as a whole. In the future, teenagers will doubtless look back with patronizing smiles at images of our smartphones and even our currency. By then, the disruptive march of artificial intelligence will be well into its stride, and that promises a further revolution not only in how we live and work, but in our evolution as a species.

Ideology

Despite our unprecedented material comforts, life in the twenty-first century is proving too much to bear for growing numbers of people. Many of the problems we are experiencing are spiritual. I mean that in the sense of being in good spirits or poor spirits: of feeling purposeful and fulfilled, or nihilistic and despairing. While the majority of people are materially better off than ever before, a large portion are caught in a global epidemic of depression and anxiety.

Around 800,000 people die by suicide per year—that's one every forty seconds.[2] This figure does not include suicide *attempts*, which can be twenty times more frequent. Suicide is now among the three leading causes of death among 15- to 44-year-olds. The highest rates used to be among elderly men. Not anymore—suicide is the second leading cause of death for young people aged 15–29. A dark corollary is the pandemic of addiction, which is engulfing people of all backgrounds and circumstances. Fed by a ruthless trade in prescription and street drugs, the toll in physical and mental suffering is unconscionable. Mental illness rates in young people are rising at an exponential rate, and there are many reasons for this, including negative media influence and a constant barrage of unrealistic expectations, socioeconomic risk factors including poverty, and the ever-rising cost of living, as well as the continued stigma and lack of understanding of mental illness in general. Another leading cause is the exhausting stress imposed upon the young by mainstream education and the pressures of standardized testing.[3]

The World We Are Destroying

There is another set of circumstances we find ourselves having to navigate with urgency: the accumulating impact of our behavior on Earth is taking a deadly toll on the planet. For the majority of human history, we have taken from the Earth without much thought for anything other than our own gain. We have stripped the planet of the natural habitats so many creatures depend on; we have wiped out species after species with hardly a glance backward. We have mined for oil, filled the air with hazardous gases, burned holes in the ozone layer, and severely depleted essential topsoil. We have filled the ground with garbage that will lie there indefinitely, and we have pumped the oceans full of toxic waste.

It hasn't always been this intense or relentless. For centuries we took what we needed to survive in small quantities—in many communities, people owned farms that they lived off, and from which they supplied their local area. International travel was a long and arduous affair, only embarked upon when necessary. People didn't hop from one continent to another for the weekend. As technology advanced and populations grew, our wants and needs advanced along with them. We are now reaching the point of no return, with some estimates grimly declaring we've already gone too far. Human behavior has changed the very chemistry of the planet, and we find ourselves at real risk of depleting the Earth of all of its resources and, in doing so, wiping ourselves from existence.

It is often said that we have to "save the planet." I'm not so sure that's true—the planet has a long time left to run until it crashes into the Sun. What we mean when we talk about saving the planet is that we have to save our own existence on it. That much is certain. If we continue to ravage the Earth at the current rate, we face no future as a species. Extinctions are a very real part of nature, but at this rate humans will join an elite and unfortunate club of species directly responsible for their own extinction.

Crosscurrents

Part of why we don't live in the world as other creatures do is that we have ideas and theories that affect what we make of it all. We see the world through various veils and lenses of values, beliefs, and ideas. As the great cultural theorist Clifford Geertz put it, we are "suspended in webs of significance [we ourselves] have spun." When we live closely with other people, we affect each other's ways of thinking and feeling. As children learn to speak, they absorb the cultural ideas and values that are embedded in those languages. In this way, they come to live in a world that's populated with beliefs, theories, and knowledge.

The richness of diversity in our cultures comes with dark complications, and a long history of human conflict driven by perceived differences. Differences in cultural beliefs can breed hostility, even hatred. When cultures collide, the turbulence can be profound and often violent. Some social disruptions are both inevitable and essential to moving humanity forward from the systemic inequalities that have haunted our pasts and threaten our futures. It is crucial to differentiate between the necessary dismantling of harmful aspects of the status quo in the name of progress, and the deadly conflicts that rage both unnecessarily and incessantly. The ability to recognize the difference between the two is directly linked to education—not just the years that most children spend in school, but through a commitment to lifelong learning and betterment.

Crosscurrents don't move in straight lines, and neither will the future. For example, the world population is not going to rise indefinitely. Already the populations of the older industrialized economies are shrinking. For 150 years, global birth rates exceeded the death rate. In the past fifty years, the global birth rate has been slowing down: in 1950 women were having an average of 4.7 children in their lifetime, by 2017 the rate had almost halved to 2.4, and it is projected to fall to below 1.7 by the end of the century.[4] One reason is education. The better women's access to education, the more active they become in managing their own fertility—and they are having fewer babies. The whole profile of the world's population will change radically during the course of this century: fewer babies and longer life expectancy mean that by 2100 the number of children under the age of 5 will be drastically lower, while the number of people over 80 will be significantly higher.

Of the population that does continue, it is almost impossible to predict what sorts of jobs they will be doing in the future, assuming they have a job at all—or, indeed, what kinds of lives they will be living. It can take a long time for the impact of technologies to permeate life and work, but the rate of change we are experiencing and the implications of the new technologies we are creating is exceptional. These developments are changing the context in which we educate people and the type of life we're educating them for, and it is imperative that we transform education accordingly.

Time for a Global Reimagining

When the status quo has existed for long enough, it's easy to believe it is unchangeable. The systems we often take for granted—political systems, how we structure our companies, the way our cities are designed—are all human-made systems. We created them to suit our purposes, to solve our problems or facilitate advancements. The problem is that as a species we have progressed to the point where many of our systems are now outdated or entirely obsolete. The good news is that it is within our powers to do something about it. We create the worlds in which we live, and there is always the possibility of re-creation.

I said earlier that we are at a critical pass. This is true. The challenges we face in our time are real and urgent, and they are all the result of human creativity. To meet these challenges, we have to harness our creativity to a more compassionate and sustainable vision of the world we want to live in, and the lives we hope to lead. It is not enough to simply do more of what we have done in the past. The answers we need are not behind us. The solution now is to cultivate our creativity with a more determined sense of purpose. That has to begin from a richer conception of our natural capacities and potential. Let's start there.

3

You're More Than You Think

**Intelligence is diverse, dynamic, and distinct.
Intelligence and creativity are blood relatives.
One cannot exist without the other.**

Children are born with boundless potential. Newborns may seem helpless, but they soon develop abilities that are unique to our species. If the conditions are right, they undergo a miraculous metamorphosis from birth to maturity. They develop physically, cognitively, emotionally, and socially, and these are all connected.

The human brain contains over 85 billion neurons. Like humanity, these neurons can form countless connections. It remains largely a mystery how this small ball of flesh and blood can give rise to the music of Mozart, the insights of Einstein, and the poetic wisdom of Maya Angelou, and to all the thoughts and feelings that constitute your own consciousness.

Take language. By the time humans are two or three years old, most learn to speak. If you are a parent, you know that you don't teach them how to do it. You don't have the time and they wouldn't have the patience. Infants know intuitively that speech sounds have meaning. They learn to speak because they want to and because they can. If they're exposed to several languages when they're young, they'll learn all of them in some capacity. Some people effortlessly speak four or five languages, usually because they lived in communities where those languages were spoken, and they have absorbed them with little effort. Most of us could speak several languages if we were immersed in them at the right time. The fact that the majority don't is a matter of circumstance, not capacity.

There's a difference between having a capacity for something and having an ability in it. An ability is a refined capacity. Language is one example of children's vast capacities. They have numerous others, some of which they will develop, many of which they may not, according to circumstances. Human resources are like natural resources. They are stunningly diverse, which is why human accomplishments are so multifarious. They are often hidden beneath the surface and have to be discovered. If they are discovered, they have to be developed to be of use.

We often greatly underestimate our children's natural capacities. In fact, we underestimate, or take for granted, rather a lot. Take our physical senses. How many do you have? Most able-bodied people would say five: hearing, sight, touch, taste, and smell. The fact is there are at least nine. They include a sense of temperature (*thermoception*), pain (*nociception*), balance (*equilibrioception*), and orientation in space (*proprioception*). These are not elite senses that only a few people have. We all depend on them all of the time. Why do we think we have five and strain to identify any others? It's because we've heard it so often that we don't think about it anymore. If we underestimate something as straightforward as our senses, what about more complex capacities like intelligence?

Ask most people about intelligence and the conversation usually turns to academic ability and IQ (Intelligence Quotient).

"Academic" is often used interchangeably with "intelligent," but while academic ability is an important example of intelligence, it is far from being the whole of it. Academic work is a mode of analysis that can be applied to anything. It refers to intellectual work that is mainly theoretical or scholarly, rather than practical or applied. Working academically generally focuses on three areas: propositional knowledge—facts about what is the case, for example, "George Washington was president of the United States of America from 1789 to 1797"; critical analysis—the impact of Washington's presidency and the nature of his leadership; and desk studies—which mainly involve reading and writing, processing and presenting facts, and critical analysis. In truth, there is no such thing as an academic subject, only academic ways of looking at things. It is not *what* is being studied, but *how* it is being studied. You can take an academic approach to anything—you can study dance without ever moving your body, you can master the concepts of art without ever creating a work yourself, you can understand chemistry without ever reaching for a test tube or lab coat.

IQ, on the other hand, proposes that we are born with a set amount of intelligence, which can be assessed through pencil-and-paper tests and given a number. We'll explore below why the fundamental assumption of IQ is wrong, but it's another good example of a system that was created a long time ago, to suit a specific purpose. The IQ system of testing as we still know it today was created in Paris at the turn of the twentieth century by Alfred Binet. At the time, Binet was working with elementary school children and was looking for a way to identify those who might require special educational support. He needed an easy-to-administer, pragmatic approach that would provide a quick diagnostic, and his system was just about as effective as he felt it needed to be. Over time, his method began to spread around the world, and in 1912 German psychologist William Stern proposed implementing a formal calculation of mental age divided by chronological age multiplied by 100 to determine a specific IQ figure. The concept of IQ was eventually picked up by members of the eugenics movement, who used it as grounds for their belief in selective breeding and population control. Their argument was that the IQ test could be used to identify people with low intelligence and stop them from reproducing. It caught on—some states in the USA legalized the sterilization of people deemed to have low intelligence, and eugenics was a key tactic of the Nazis' Final Solution.

Like Gutenberg with his press, or Jobs with the iPhone, Binet could not have anticipated the consequences of the IQ test. He certainly would not have imagined that a century later it would be synonymous with intelligence itself. That's because while IQ may tell us something about intelligence, it doesn't tell us every-thing. In many respects, it doesn't tell us much. Intelligence is far richer: it is diverse, dynamic, and distinct.

Diverse

Intelligence is a highly cultural concept: different cultures value different aspects of intelligence over others. There is also no formally agreed-upon definition of intelligence. This is not because people haven't tried. On the contrary, psychologists have dedicated incalculable amounts of time to the subject. It is because intelligence takes multiple forms and we each have natural strengths and weaknesses in all of them. Take a look at the wondrous variety of skills and insights that drive achievements in every field of human endeavor, and the countless ways they all interact. These forms of intelligence go far beyond the pencil-and-paper conundrums of the typical IQ test.

Intelligence includes the ability to formulate and express our thoughts coherently. There are multiple ways of doing this—through speech, writing, music, dance, numbers, demonstration, drawing, among others—and we all do a variety of them, if not all of them, in various combinations at one point or another. Visual artists spend the majority of their time forming visual ideas that they then render into a physical form, but that does not mean they are incapable of forming coherent sentences. Elite mathematicians often make sense of the world using numbers, angles, and shapes, but may also move their bodies to make a point. Those are two extremes, but the majority of us use multiple ways of forming thoughts and expressing them on a daily basis.

There's more to it, such as circumstance and opportunity. I mentioned earlier that a child who grows up in a house exposed to multiple languages will learn to speak all of them. It goes both ways—that same child growing up in a house hearing only one language will speak only the one. It doesn't mean that he or she can't learn a language later on, but it won't be second nature. This is true of most things. When children are taken to dance classes from a young age, they develop a keen understanding of how their bodies work, of spatial awareness, and of stamina. If the same group of children had not been taken to dance classes, developing these understandings later in life would require a more intentional effort. So while we all use different methods to formulate and express thoughts daily, our circumstances and opportunities play a big part in which of these methods we use more often, or are more comfortable using. Which leads us nicely to the next point: intelligence is dynamic.

Dynamic

Different areas of the brain are associated with specific functions. Even so, none of them work independently of the rest of the brain, but in concert with it. Similarly, consciousness is not located exclusively in our skulls. The brain can only function through its intimate connections with the rest of the body. For example, the gut in the abdomen is lined with millions of neurons. The "gut brain" communicates with the brain through an intricate network of neurons, hormones, and chemicals that constantly provide feedback about how hungry we are, whether we're stressed or exhilarated, or if we've ingested a noxious microbe. This information superhighway is called the brain-gut axis, and it provides constant updates on the state of affairs at our two ends.

Dr. Amir Amedi is a neuroscientist based in Israel. His work involves teaching congenitally blind people to "see" using sound. By using a series of sound patterns, vibrations, tones, and noise bursts, Dr. Amedi trains his patients to identify everyday objects. Through his method, a person who has never seen before can sit at a table and pick the one green apple out of a bowl of otherwise red apples. In developing this work, Dr. Amedi conducted a series of brain scans on people with full sight to determine the difference between sight and imagination. In one scan, he showed his subject a green apple, and in the next, he asked the same subject to imagine a green apple. What these experiments found is that different parts of the brain light up depending on the situation— one area lit up when the subject was looking at an actual apple, and a different area when the same person was imagining an apple. In essence, what he proved is that there is a specific part of the brain dedicated to imagination.

Our brains are highly dynamic: each part of the brain bounces off other parts to accomplish even the most basic of tasks. Consider the act of speaking: we form thoughts in our minds and convert them to words; we often adapt what we are saying to be understood by the person we are talking to; and we control the volume and tone of our voice. We also move while we talk: we gesticulate and contort our faces to convey emotion and meaning. We then process what we have said and wait for a response. The simple art of having a conversation uses a myriad of brain functions in a concerto. In fact, the dynamism of the brain is much like an orchestra—many different individual parts playing together to create something that is only possible when they all play together in harmony.

Distinct

Babies are not blank pages. They come into the world fully loaded. As every parent knows, these innate characteristics show themselves very early on in life. If you're a parent of two or more children, I bet you they are completely different. You'd never confuse them, would you? They may look alike and have similar characteristics, or may remind you of yourself or your parents, but they are their own individual. We are all unique blends of our predecessors, from how we look to the nuances of our personalities, but every life is singular and unrepeatable.

Although every child has boundless capacities, they manifest differently in each. As children develop specific abilities, their brains are being physically shaped in response. It was once believed that we are born with a fixed amount of intelligence, and there was nothing much we could do about it. Newborns began their lives with all the brain cells they would ever have, and those cells died off over time as a natural process of aging. We now know this isn't the case. The brain is a living organ, dynamic and "plastic," and constantly evolving with experience. Much like muscle, the brain develops and changes with use. Learning generates new neural connections and pathways throughout our lives, provided our brains are active and challenged by new tasks, an essential element of human adaptability. So not only is intelligence diverse, dynamic, and distinct, it is also adaptable. We are born with vast capacities, and we have numerous opportunities to build on them across our lifetimes.

Blood Relatives

One of the fundamental issues with narrowly defining intelligence as IQ or academic ability is that it totally disregards the relationship between intelligence and creativity. It creates a divide between the two, and in doing so it divides people into groups—those who are intelligent and those who are creative. We do this in our schools when we separate the so-called "core" subjects like mathematics, literacy, and the sciences from the "soft" subjects like the arts and humanities. We also do it in our businesses when we separate the "creatives" from the rest of the company. In making these clear distinctions, we buy into and perpetuate several myths about creativity and intelligence.

One myth is that only certain people are creative, and you are therefore either creative or not. Just as we know that we aren't born with a certain amount of intelligence, we are not born with a certain amount of creativity. Creativity, like the brain or muscle, changes with use. If we neglect our creative capacities, they lie dormant. If we use them properly, they grow and develop.

Another myth is that creativity only applies to certain activities, like the arts. While it's true that the arts involve a high level of creativity, it is not true that other activities, such as mathematics, running a business, or studying the brain, do not. When Dr. Amedi was creating his method to train blind people to "see" using sound, he called upon all of his faculties, including building on his existing knowledge, generating new ideas, analysis, and design. In chapter 1 we talked about how imagination allows us to envision alternative possibilities, and creativity equips us with the tools to bring them into existence. That's exactly what Dr. Amedi did. He imagined a reality in which blind people could see, and he used his powers of creativity, combined with his scientific expertise, to make it happen. Yet neuroscience is not traditionally acknowledged as a creative subject. On the contrary, gaining the necessary qualifications to be accepted into a course to study neuroscience often requires showcasing a certain type of intelligence at the expense of any other.

You can be creative at anything that involves your intelligence. It is because of the diversity of human intelligence that we have such varied capacities for creativity. And this is because intelligence and creativity are blood relatives. You cannot be creative without acting intelligently, and the highest form of intelligence is thinking creatively. The two coexist and work in tandem.

Living in Two Worlds

We live not in one world, but in two. The first is the world around us: the exterior world of the cities and lands we live in, the people around us, material objects, events, and circumstances. The second is the world within you: the interior world of your personal consciousness. The world around you exists whether or not you do. It was there when you came into it and it will be there when you have gone. At least we hope. The world within you exists only because you do. It came into being when you did and as far as we know it will cease when you do. Our lives are formed by the constant interactions between these two worlds.

A jellyfish and a killer whale may inhabit the same stretch of ocean, but they inhabit entirely different universes because of how they are built and what they perceive of their surroundings. What's true of whales and jellyfish is true of us. If we were twelve feet tall, had wings, and could hear like dogs, life would be rather different. But human life is more than just physical: as well as having to navigate our physical circumstances, we also have to make sense of our cultural environments, as well as our own thoughts, interpretations, and emotions.

Just as children are not born as blank slates, the world they come into is dense with the insights, artifacts, and legacies of ten thousand generations of humanity. We are heirs to deep stores of human knowledge that have been wrought by countless minds, in many fields, across cultures and down the ages.

The dynamics of nature and nurture generate a huge diversity of individual talents, dispositions, and personalities. How we think about the world around us is deeply affected by the feelings within us, and how we feel is often shaped by our knowledge, perceptions, and experiences. As the writer Anaïs Nin once said, "I do not see the world as it is, I see it as I am." We all create our own lives through the perspectives we develop and the choices we make. All children are born with vast potential. Whether they fulfill that potential has everything to do with how well they flourish in both worlds, outer and inner. The quality of the education they receive is fundamental to getting those conditions right. Education should be the bridge between these two worlds. Understanding how is the foundation to making that bridge more secure for all our children.

4

The Promise of Education

Education must enable students to understand the world around them and the talents within them so that they can become fulfilled individuals and active, compassionate citizens.

What *is education for?* As it happens, people differ sharply on this question. It is what is known as an "essentially contested concept." Like "democracy" and "justice," "education" means different things to different people. Various factors can contribute to a person's understanding of the purpose of education, including their background and circumstances. It is also inflected by how they view related issues such as ethnicity, gender, and social class. Still, not having an agreed-upon definition of education doesn't mean we can't discuss it or do anything about it. We just need to be clear on terms.

There are a few terms that are often confused or used interchangeably—"learning," "education," "training," and "school"—but there are important differences between them. *Learning* is the process of acquiring new skills and understanding. *Education* is an organized system of learning. *Training* is a type of education that is focused on learning specific skills. A *school* is a community of learners: a group that comes together to learn with and from each other. It is vital that we differentiate these terms: children love to learn, they do it naturally; many have a hard time with education, and some have big problems with school.

There are many assumptions of compulsory education. One is that young people need to know, understand, and be able to do certain things that they most likely would not if they were left to their own devices. What these things are and how best to ensure students learn them are complicated and often controversial issues. Another assumption is that compulsory education is a preparation for what will come afterward, like getting a good job or going on to higher education.

So, what does it mean to be educated now? Well, I believe that education should expand our consciousness, capabilities, sensitivities, and cultural understanding. It should enlarge our worldview. As we all live in two worlds—the world within you that exists only because you do, and the world around you—the core purpose of education is to enable students to understand both worlds. In today's climate, there is also a new and urgent challenge: to provide forms of education that engage young people with the global-economic issues of environmental well-being.

This core purpose of education can be broken down into the following four basic purposes.

Personal

Education should enable young people to engage with the world within them as well as the world around them. In Western cultures, there is a firm distinction between the two worlds, between thinking and feeling, objectivity and subjectivity. This distinction is misguided. There is a deep correlation between our experience of the world around us and how we feel. As we explored in the previous chapters, all individuals have unique strengths and weaknesses, outlooks and personalities. Students do not come in standard physical shapes, nor do their abilities and personalities. They all have their own aptitudes and dispositions and different ways of understanding things. Education is therefore deeply personal. It is about cultivating the minds and hearts of living people. Engaging them as individuals is at the heart of raising achievement.

The Universal Declaration of Human Rights emphasizes that "all human beings are born free and equal in dignity and rights," and that "education shall be directed to the full development of the human personality and to the strengthening of respect for human rights and fundamental freedoms." Many of the deepest problems in current systems of education result from losing sight of this basic principle.

Cultural

Schools should enable students to understand their own cultures and to respect the diversity of others. There are various definitions of culture, but in this context the most appropriate is "the values and forms of behavior that characterize different social groups." To put it more bluntly, it is "the way we do things around here." Education is one of the ways that communities pass on their values from one generation to the next. For some, education is a way of preserving a culture against outside influences. For others, it is a way of promoting cultural tolerance. As the world becomes more crowded and connected, it is becoming more complex culturally. Living respectfully with diversity is not just an ethical choice, it is a practical imperative.

There should be three cultural priorities for schools: to help students understand their own cultures, to understand other cultures, and to promote a sense of cultural tolerance and coexistence. The lives of all communities can be hugely enriched by celebrating their own cultures and the practices and traditions of other cultures.

Economic

Education should enable students to become economically responsible and independent. This is one of the reasons governments take such a keen interest in education: they know that an educated workforce is essential to creating economic prosperity. Leaders of the Industrial Revolution knew that education was critical to creating the type of workforce they required too. But the world of work has changed so profoundly since then, and continues to do so at an ever-quickening pace. We know that many of the jobs of previous decades are disappearing and being rapidly replaced by contemporary counterparts. It is almost impossible to predict the direction of advancing technologies, and where they will take us.

How can schools prepare students to navigate this ever-changing economic landscape? They must connect students with their unique talents and interests, dissolve the division between academic and vocational programs, and foster practical partnerships between schools and the world of work, so that young people can experience working environments as part of their education, not simply when it is time for them to enter the labor market.

Social

Education should enable young people to become active and compassionate citizens. We live in densely woven social systems. The benefits we derive from them depend on our working together to sustain them. The empowerment of individuals has to be balanced by practicing the values and responsibilities of collective life, and of democracy in particular. Our freedoms in democratic societies are not automatic. They come from centuries of struggle against tyranny and autocracy and those who foment sectarianism, hatred, and fear. Those struggles are far from over. As John Dewey observed, "Democracy has to be born anew every generation, and education is its midwife."

For a democratic society to function, it depends upon the majority of its people to be active within the democratic process. In many democracies, this is increasingly not the case. Schools should engage students in becoming active, and proactive, democratic participants. An academic civics course will scratch the surface, but to nurture a deeply rooted respect for democracy, it is essential to give young people real-life democratic experiences long before they come of age to vote.

Eight Core Competencies

The conventional curriculum is based on a collection of separate subjects. These are prioritized according to beliefs around the limited understanding of intelligence we discussed in the previous chapter, as well as what is deemed to be important later in life. The idea of "subjects" suggests that each subject, whether mathematics, science, art, or language, stands completely separate from all the other subjects. This is problematic. Mathematics, for example, is not defined only by propositional knowledge; it is a combination of types of knowledge, including concepts, processes, and methods as well as propositional knowledge. This is also true of science, art, and languages, and of all other subjects. It is therefore much more useful to focus on the concept of disciplines rather than subjects.

Disciplines are fluid; they constantly merge and collaborate. In focusing on disciplines rather than subjects we can also explore the concept of interdisciplinary learning. This is a much more holistic approach that mirrors real life more closely—it is rare that activities outside of school are as clearly segregated as conventional curriculums suggest. A journalist writing an article, for example, must be able to call upon skills of conversation, deductive reasoning, literacy, and social sciences. A surgeon must understand the academic concept of the patient's condition as well as the practical application of the appropriate procedure. At least, we would certainly hope this is the case should we find ourselves being wheeled into surgery.

The concept of disciplines brings us to a better starting point when planning the curriculum, which is to ask what students should know and be able to do as a result of their education. The four purposes above suggest eight core competencies that, if properly integrated into education, will equip students who leave school to engage in the personal, cultural, economic, and social challenges they will inevitably face in their lives. These competencies are curiosity, creativity, criticism, communication, collaboration, compassion, composure, and citizenship. Rather than be triggered by age, these competencies should be interwoven from the beginning of a student's educational journey and nurtured throughout.

Curiosity — *the ability to ask questions and explore how the world works*

Babies are born deeply curious. It is curiosity that takes them from tiny, helpless creatures, dependent upon their parents for every waking (and sleeping) need, to independent toddlers. It is curiosity that inclines these toddlers to ask more questions than most parents have answers to. Curiosity is our most comprehensive learning tool in the first years of life.

Every step forward humanity has taken has been driven by

the inherent desire to explore, to question how things work, to wonder why, and to dare to "imagine if . . ." Children are awash with natural curiosity, and when their curiosity is engaged they will learn for themselves, from each other, and from a multitude of other sources. Great teachers nurture and guide this curiosity: they provoke interest and scaffold exploration.

Creativity — *the ability to generate new ideas and to apply them in practice*

As the challenges facing young people proliferate, it is essential to help them develop their unique creative capacities. Like imagination, creativity is not a single power located in one part of our brains but an overall power that arises from the complex functions of our minds as a whole. Creativity is possible in all areas of human life. It can be cultivated and refined, which involves an increasing mastery of skills, knowledge, and ideas. Creative work in any domain involves increasing control of the knowledge, concepts, and practices that have shaped that domain and a deepening understanding of the traditions and achievements in which it is based.

Criticism — *the ability to analyze information and ideas and to form reasoned arguments and judgments*

One of the hallmarks of human intelligence is our ability to consider arguments logically and weigh evidence dispassionately. Our flourishing as humans has always been dependent on these abilities of critical thinking, but the challenges we are currently facing make it even more imperative. Young people in particular are now bombarded from every direction with pitches for their attention. The line between fact and fiction, between trustworthy sources and propaganda masked as clickbait, is fading. Finding the truth in a sea of deception is becoming an increasingly difficult daily task, and one we must help our young people master. Critical thinking should be at the heart of every discipline in school.

Communication— *the ability to express thoughts and feelings clearly and confidently in a range of media and forms*

Communication is not only about words and numbers. We think and communicate about the world in all the ways we experience it. We think in sounds and images, in movement, and in all the ways they make possible, like music, poetry, and dance. We also think in metaphors and analogies: we reason and empathize; speculate and suppose; imagine and create. Fluency in reading, writing, and mathematics are accepted imperatives in education and so they should be. It is just as important to promote clear and confident speech. Verbal communication is not only about literal meanings: it is about appreciating metaphor, analogy, allusion, and other poetic and literary forms of language. Being able to form and communicate thoughts and feelings is fundamental to both personal well-being and collective achievement and collaboration.

Collaboration— *the ability to work constructively with others*

The human adventure can only be carried forward through complex forms of collaboration. Without the ability to work with others we would stand no chance against the challenges we collectively face. Fortunately, human beings are social creatures: we live and learn in the company of others. This is true in most situations, but seldom cultivated in school environments. Too often, young people learn *in* groups but not *as* groups. Working as a group creates opportunities for problem solving and meeting common goals. By drawing on each other's strengths, mitigating weaknesses, and sharing ideas, students learn to resolve conflicts and to support agreed solutions.

Compassion— *the ability to empathize with others and to act accordingly*

Empathy is identifying with the feelings of others and imagining how we would feel in similar circumstances. Compassion is the practice of empathy. Many problems that young people face, such as bullying, violence, and prejudice, are rooted in lack of compassion. In the adult world, cultural conflicts and toxic social divisions are inflamed by it. As the world becomes more interdependent, cultivating compassion is a moral and a practical imperative. It is also a spiritual commitment to treat others as you would have them treat you. Practicing compassion is the truest expression of our common humanity and can be a deep source of happiness in ourselves and in others.

Composure— *the ability to connect with the inner life of feeling and develop a sense of personal harmony and balance*

Many young people suffer from anxiety and depression in school for a variety of reasons—some having to do with school itself and others caused by situations outside of it. One of the many reasons a school should not exist in a vacuum is that personal lives are sucked in whether or not they are acknowledged. Not acknowledging them, and piling additional stress on top in the form of excess homework or exam pressure, can lead to disengagement, anger, and worse. Schools can mitigate the effects by transforming their cultures to take a holistic approach to each child. They can also give students the time and techniques to explore their inner worlds through the daily practice of mindfulness and meditation. A growing number of schools are doing this, and students and faculty alike are feeling the benefits.

Citizenship— *the ability to engage constructively with society and to participate in the processes that sustain it*

Engaged citizens are capable of having an influence on the world when they are active in their communities and responsible for their own actions. Schools have vital roles in cultivating that sense of citizenship. This means educating young people on their rights and responsibilities, informing them about how social and political systems work, nurturing their concern for the welfare of others, and creating opportunities for them to voice their opinions and arguments, as well as creating real-world experiences of the democratic process throughout their education. Childhood is not a rehearsal. Young people are living their lives now, and who they become and what they do in the future has everything to do with what they experience in the present. The skills of citizenship need to be practiced and continually renewed.

A Contemporary Education

These four purposes and eight competencies are essential aspects of being human. They are no more or less than what we expect of each adult we encounter in both our professional and personal lives. Despite the widely acknowledged, and frankly unignorable, changes societies around the world continue to experience, education systems generally remain rooted in the past. The answer is not simply to do more of what has always been done. The solutions we require are not in the rearview mirror. The challenge is not to reform our systems but to transform them. In order to effectively raise children who will thrive in the world they are inheriting, we must revolutionize education. The revolution we need involves rethinking how schools work.

5

From the Factory to the Farm

We are depleting our human resources in the same way we are depleting Earth's resources. Our future depends on tackling both crises urgently.

Traditional methods of formal education are often compared to an industrial factory. In this analogy, children are the commodity being manufactured in a linear process along a conveyor belt; teachers are the factory workers, each responsible for their own section; and along the way, there are a series of quality control checks. The whole process is routine, predefined, and regulated. You can see why this has caught on as an image—the shared goal of mass production and most major education systems is the creation of a standardized final product, and the methods they use to achieve it are remarkably similar.

The factory analogy highlights many aspects of what is wrong with mainstream education. However, people are not inanimate objects. Inanimate objects, whether screws or airplanes, have no opinions or feelings about how they are produced or what happens to them. People do. They have feelings, motivations, concerns, personal circumstances, and talents. They are invested in what happens to them, and what happens to them shapes who they are. This is as true of children as of adults. Contrary to popular belief, life does not begin at eighteen, or when graduating high schoolers cross the stage to collect their diplomas. It begins long before the final "product" is packed up and shipped off.

The Industrial Revolution sparked unprecedented innovations in energy, manufacturing, transport, agriculture, hygiene, and medicine. It also sparked the mass systems of education that we know today, and modeled them in its own image to suit its own purposes. It stands to follow that an industrial model of education would share similarities with industrial factories, and it does. However, the proper analogy for industrial education is not the manufacture of inanimate objects, but the industrial production of living things. It is not an industrial factory, but an industrial farm.

Industrial Farming

The Industrial Revolution redefined normal. The progress it made in manufacturing and technology created a lasting change in agriculture. Mechanization made it possible to plow huge tracts of land, which yielded great monocultures—vast fields of one type of crop. Chemical fertilizers were introduced at scale to "protect" the crops in these unnatural environments from the natural ecosystems that gravitate toward them. In doing so, they also devastated food chains of insects that feed on the crops, and small animals and birds that feed on the seeds and insects.

The Industrial Revolution took a similar approach to farming livestock, implementing factory farms in place of open grazing. Huge numbers of animals began to be raised indoors, often with little to no access to the outside world during their lifetimes. As with crops, the industrial production of animal products is intended to maximize production at minimal financial cost.

The wider cost to human and planetary health has been significant, and we are only just beginning to fully understand the long-term implications. For example, animal production in industrial conditions depends on the widespread use of powerful antibiotics. These are used for a variety of purposes in raising livestock, including the treatment of sick animals, the prevention of illness in healthy animals, and to boost animal growth.[1] In fact, the animal products sector accounts for approximately 80 percent of the world's consumption of antibiotics,[2] which more often than not are administered to healthy animals rather than sick ones. This misuse of antibiotics is a contributing factor in the global rise of antibiotic resistance, a phenomenon the World Health Organization describes as "one of the biggest threats to global health, food security, and development today."[3] The issue is not that we human beings become resistant ourselves, but that bacteria do. When we become infected with antibiotic-resistant bacteria and we become ill, the infections are much harder to treat—leading to longer illnesses, extended hospital stays, and higher mortality rates. Not only are antibiotic-resistant bacteria commonly found in the meat we consume, but there is also a mound of evidence that these bacteria can be found in the air inside and surrounding industrial farms, in the water of rivers and streams, on the backs of flies, and even blowing off the backs of vehicles transporting livestock,[4] meaning our risk of exposure is increasingly high. Unnecessarily so.

Another lasting consequence of industrial farming is that the increase in yield made possible by these systems of production led to an increase in appetite. As a result, an unnatural abundance of cows, pigs, sheep, and poultry are constantly bred to keep up with demand. The increase in breeding of certain species has caused the casual eradication of thousands of other species that we find less appetizing, some by deliberate extermination, most as the collateral damage of humanity's self-absorbed way of life. Additionally, keeping huge numbers of livestock massively contributes to the rising greenhouse gases heating the planet, with some leading estimates holding livestock agriculture responsible for 30 percent to 51 percent of all greenhouse gas emissions produced.[5]

Industrial production is ravaging natural habitats, degrading soils, and poisoning the oceans. We are destroying ancient ecosystems and vital food chains on which all life depends, including our own. Most of us now live in cities, another by-product of the Industrial Revolution, and as such it's easy to forget that we are part of nature and depend on its health for our own.

There are deep parallels between the ways in which we are stripping the Earth of its critically diverse natural resources and the implications of our social systems, which are stripping away our diversity of human resources—in particular, our education systems.

As the ocean depends upon the vast variety of fish and plant life it houses to sustain its delicate balance, our human ecosystem depends upon the variety of talents and skill sets we possess to nurture our ever complicated and complex ways of living. However, in the same way industrial farming is depleting the ocean of its vital inhabitants through devastating trawling and unconscionable amounts of bycatch—fish or other life caught unintentionally while fishing and thrown back into the ocean to die—our education systems are depleting our innate diversity of talents through prioritizing a small cross section of skills and subjects deemed to be more important than others, and throwing the rest aside.

Industrial Education

The Industrial Revolution required a specific type of education system for a specific outcome—a tiered workforce. As such, the system it created was also tiered, and designed to prepare a small number of students to go on to administrative and professional occupations, a larger number to take up trade, and the majority for blue-collar jobs. Industrialism needed a lot more manual workers than university graduates, and as such the system was designed as a pyramid to meet this need.

Despite the astronomical changes in circumstances between the Industrial Revolution and the twenty-first century, formal systems of education by and large remain structurally the same. Students and teachers spend huge amounts of their time in conditions that have been designed for the mass production of a standardized product, the student, that by design focuses on output and yield. While industrial farms prioritize quantity, size, and cost over quality, health, and natural ecosystems, we prioritize test data, attendance, and college admission over well-being, creativity, and learning. While industrial farms pump crops and livestock with vast amounts of antibiotics, we prescribe mood-stabilizing and attention-enhancing drugs to children to compensate for the very real levels of anxiety, stress, and disengagement they are experiencing.

This is not without consequence. Depression is the fourth leading cause of illness and disability among adolescents aged 15–19 years, and fifteenth for those aged 10–14 years.[6] There are many various and complicated factors that contribute to these statistics, including trauma, abuse, illness, and poverty. It also cannot be overlooked that if children are made to sit for hours on end, day after day, doing work they find uninteresting, for tests they find intimidating, to prepare for some future goal they find uninspiring, that they may fidget and become anxious, stressed, or disengaged.

Like the majority of its systems, the Industrial Revolution's design of education was based on conformity. The problem with conformity in education is that people are not standardized to begin with. Challenging the idea of conformity in schools does not mean to advocate for antisocial behavior. All communities depend upon agreed conventions of conduct. To challenge conformity in education means to dispute the institutional tendency to judge students by a single standard of ability. In this sense, the alternative to conformity is to celebrate diversity. Until we begin to fully celebrate the vibrant diversity that makes our species so unique, we will continue to deplete our human resources much as we are depleting the Earth's natural resources. If we do not change our course on both, the repercussions will be disastrous. We can take lessons from one and apply them to the other.

Regenerative Farming

Scientists largely agree that industrial systems of agriculture are unsustainable. The Earth simply does not have enough resources to cater to the demand we place on it. The good news is that there are growing movements in regenerative farming and rewilding, and there are big differences from the industrial models in how they fundamentally operate. Rather than focusing on standardization, they prioritize diversity.

Regenerative farmers prioritize the ecosystem. They focus first and foremost on the soil. Soil is a rich, life-giving ecosystem in and of itself. If the soil is healthy, life will flourish indefinitely. From healthy soil a variety of crops are grown in proximities so they can create their own natural protection. The crops then create conditions in which the insects and wildlife that depend upon them flourish. Regenerative farmers follow the seasons and have natural crop rotation cycles. The same approach is taken in the treatment of animals, which roam on pastures. In letting grazing animals roam, not only are they provided with all they need, they also play a vital role in retaining grasslands, which in turn sustains pollinating insects, absorbs water, and helps to keep the ecosystem thriving by maintaining the health of the soil.

Rewilding is the process of restoring natural ecosystems to the point where they can take care of themselves, and it involves setting large sections of land, forest, or sea aside as protected areas. It can also involve the reintroduction of key species in order to help the ecosystem. At its core, rewilding gives the natural world a much-needed break from human intervention, including hunting, logging, or fishing, so that it has the opportunity to rebuild. And it does rebuild. One of the most incredible aspects of the natural world is its ability to heal. Life always finds a way. Take Chernobyl: less than fifty years since the worst nuclear disaster in human history, the city that was evacuated within twenty-four hours and left untouched is now a thriving ecosystem of natural life. The images are striking—large trees growing through buildings and endangered animals roaming freely among deserted streets.

There are other, more intentional and less devastating examples of rewilding, the most famous of which is the reintroduction of wolves to Yellowstone National Park in the 1990s. In the 1800s wolves were eradicated from their natural habitat, mostly due to agriculture. In their absence, deer began to overpopulate and overrun the park, destroying much of the plant life through their overgrazing. When the wolves were reintroduced, they not only culled the deer population, they also changed the deer's behavior, causing them to stay away from sections of the park entirely. Free from the constantly feasting deer, trees were able to grow to their full height, plants began to flower, smaller creatures fed on the increase of berries, and in turn eagles and hawks returned to feed on them. The ground became healthier, and riverbanks strengthened. Yellowstone began to thrive again.

It's important to note that the reason rewilding is essential to the future of our planet is because our industrial systems are responsible for the degradation of natural habitats and ecosystems. In a sense, there is no way to rewild; we cannot reclaim the Eden of the natural world in its entirety. But we can re-create the conditions for life to recover and, in doing so, reverse large portions of the damage we are responsible for.

What both regenerative farming and rewilding practices have in common is a respect for ecosystems. They create the conditions for life to flourish and then take a step back and watch as it does. There is a synergy here with what needs to happen in our education systems.

Rewilding Education

Much like the agricultural systems that thrive when the soil is right, we thrive when the culture is right. An education system is not successful because of tests and output-driven hurdles; it is successful when individuals are recognized, and the diversity of their talent is celebrated. It is successful when students are fulfilled and continue to live fulfilling lives.

Schools are part of wider cultural ecosystems, and in the same way great farmers nurture a plant's natural ecosystems, great schools nurture their connections with the wider communities of which they are a part. They also make creative connections within the school itself; they approach learning in ways that are cross-age, cross-curricular, and multidisciplinary. Rather than raising generations of monocultures, they encourage a mixed culture of the sciences, the arts, technology, of individual passions, and the unique pathways they each determine.

Education will only truly progress when we understand and recognize that it too is a living system, and that the art is to invigorate the living culture of schools themselves. Just as skillful farmers focus on the soil to create the conditions for plants to grow and flourish, skillful schools focus on creating the conditions for children to grow and flourish. So, what does that look like in practice?

6

Creating Miracles

Our role is to create the right conditions for life and learning to flourish. When we do that, we realize we have been in the miracle business all along.

A system is a set of related processes that have a combined effect. There are many different types of systems, ranging from simple to complex. A lever, for example, is a simple system—it is a rigid bar with a pivot closer to one end. When force is applied to the long end it creates a greater force at the short end. Complicated systems are made up of many simple systems that are designed to work together, like a computer, an oven, or a mechanical crane.

Living systems like plants, animals, and people, however, are not only complicated systems, they are complex. Living organisms comprise many systems that appear to be completely separate but that are in fact intimately related, each depending on every other to sustain the health of the whole organism. A flower with damaged roots will not flourish. Living systems are also dependent on the health of their environment to sustain their own maximum health: a tree that has stood for hundreds of years may die during a sudden period of drought or particularly intense winds. Still, living systems are also capable of adapting and evolving. Their relationship with their physical environment is dynamic. For example, trees in areas of dense shade have been known to create a partnership called *mycorrhiza* between their roots and certain fungi in the soil to nourish neighboring trees. The phenomenon, known as the "wood wide web," allows hub trees to send nutrients from one tree to another, and in doing so create a lifeline for those trees unable to reach the sunlight.

Education is a complex adaptive and living system—there are multiple systems within the system, which constantly interact with each other to keep the whole thing going. The "simple" systems that contribute to the whole include individual schools and departments, social services, student counseling and psychological services, health care, and examinations and testing agencies. Additionally, there are numerous interest groups, including students, parents, educators, employers, professional and commercial organizations, publishers, testing agencies, and politicians. Education exists through the real actions of very real people. As such, it is constantly adapting and evolving in the face of new technologies, political climates, and global events. Because education is adaptive and living, it can change, and because the climate and conditions that it exists within have changed so much, it has to.

A Community of Learners

An ecosystem is another complex adaptive system, it is a "biological community of interacting organisms and their physical environment." While ecosystems traditionally refer to the natural world—to coral reefs and rainforests, for instance—a school is very much an ecosystem. Every school is a living community of people interacting through their relationships, experiences, and feelings. The many different systems, including admissions, maintenance, business development, governors or PTAs, student welfare representatives, and subject departments, all depend upon each other to be working properly for the whole school to flourish. The curriculum and schedule may be meticulously planned, but if the building is crumbling, the experience will be affected. On the other hand, it may have an outstanding campus with world-class facilities, but if there is a culture of bullying the environment will become toxic.

Schools are also part of wider cultural ecosystems. They are not set apart from the turmoil of everyday life—they are embroiled in the world around them in every way. In particular, schools make up the wider education system and as such are directly affected by it. If the overwhelming priority of an education system is to focus on high-stakes assessment, its schools will naturally take the burden. If the wider system sees students as data points, it runs the risk of students seeing themselves that way too. If the political climate is weighted in certain directions, such as test results and college admissions, an individual school will struggle to find resources for other priorities.

So how can we fix a system that is no longer fit for purpose? Let's start by looking at individual schools, using the definition from chapter 4: a community of learners, a group that comes together to learn with and from each other. This can include any learning community, including private, state, compulsory, voluntary, home schoolers, or unschoolers.

Invigorate the Living Culture

Great environmentalists know that the best way to let the natural world heal is to create the conditions for ecosystems to thrive. Left to its own devices, the Earth knows how to get life going—its default position is life. Poor conservation efforts do the opposite: they ignore natural biodiversity and dictate every aspect from the height of the grass to the location of each plant, to which species are allowed near it and how often. The result may look pretty from the outside, but a closer inspection discovers a poor imitation of nature. These conservation efforts focus on the outcome, not the process.

There is a parallel here with education reform movements. Reform movements ignore the natural diversity of human talents and dictate every aspect of schooling, from reading lists to classroom layout to scheduling. The result may look pretty from the outside, but a closer inspection discovers a poor imitation of learning. They focus too much on the outcome, on test scores and graduation rates, rather than on the process.

The default position of children is to learn. If students are not learning, education is not happening. The core purpose of a school, then, is to create optimal conditions for learning to happen. In achieving this, we must invigorate the living culture of schools themselves by focusing on creating the conditions for ecosystems to thrive. The key to a thriving ecosystem is diversity. As luck would have it, schools are rich ground for diversity. So what does a thriving school ecosystem look like?

It Values Its Teachers

At the heart of education is the relationship between teachers and students. Schools, and education systems more widely, make a critical error when they disregard the value of teachers. Some of the major education systems in the world undertrain, underpay, and undervalue their teachers. They cast teachers in the role of service workers, whose job is to "deliver" standards as though they were a branch of FedEx. These systems micromanage their teachers, in some cases even linking their job security to student performance: if the children pass, so do they. All the while, their opinions and professional expertise are systematically ignored. Thriving education systems, on the other hand, put huge value on the importance of well-trained, highly motivated, and well-compensated teachers. Teachers are trusted with their work and treated as the professionals they are.

Teaching is an art form. Great teachers use a wide repertory of approaches, from direct instruction to scaffolded activities, and like all genuine professionals, they use their judgment and connoisseurship to know which method to deploy depending on each specific situation. Effective teaching is a constant process of adjustment, judgment, and response. In their various roles, teachers inspire students with their own passion; they help students acquire the skills and knowledge they need to become confident, independent learners; and they enable students to inquire, ask questions, and develop the skills and disposition of original thinking.

A healthy school ecosystem empowers its teachers, encourages them, and nurtures their growth and development.

It Is Interdisciplinary

In chapter 4 we looked at the idea of *disciplines* rather than subjects. One of the problems with grouping by subject is that it implies different areas of the curriculum are defined only by their subject matter. A common assumption, for example, is that the sciences and the arts are complete opposites in education. It is assumed that the sciences are about truth, objectivity, and hard facts alone; in contrast, the arts are only concerned with feelings, creativity, and subjectivity. In reality, the arts and sciences have all sorts of crossovers. All great discoveries that have driven science forward have depended on profound leaps of imagination combined with practical ingenuity of experiments, and the arts are highly disciplined forms of practice that call upon refined skills and critical judgment.

The concept of *disciplines* instead of subjects opens up the dynamics of interdisciplinary work. It allows for the natural cross-pollination between all aspects of the curriculum in a way that is much more reflective of real life. Outside of schools, disciplines shift and evolve: they are dynamic fields of inquiry. It should be this way within schools too.

It Mixes Age Groups

In all the ways we have explored, each child thinks, behaves, and learns differently. While there are various benchmarks most children hit at around the same time, such as walking and talking or puberty, if you are a parent you know that every child is on their own track of development. Children learn different things at different paces: one child may be a keen reader at an early age but be slower to fine-tune gross motor skills. Another may grasp concepts of science easily but require more support with communication skills.

In traditional schools, children are taught in specific age groups—all of the seven-year-olds together in one group, separate from all of the nine-year-olds. From an administrative point of view, this makes sense. It also makes sense from the perspective of industrial priorities. However, when it comes to what and how children actually learn, segregation by age makes little sense at all.

When children of different ages learn together, they can be grouped by their stage of mastery rather than their chronological age. The younger students can benefit from the relative sophistication of the older ones, who reinforce their own learning by helping the younger ones. In bringing a variety of ages together, the experience, knowledge, and ability of each is enhanced. It also provides opportunities for children to nurture each other, developing empathy, responsibility, and patience.

Breaking the age barrier in this way also creates organic opportunities for teachers to learn from students, which benefits both parties. When done authentically, students feel empowered and respected, while teachers learn from perspectives they may not have considered.

It Personalizes Learning

You cannot force a person to learn. It is a deeply personal act and has to be personalized to be fully effective. There is an argument from some that personalizing education for every student is impossible. They say it would be too expensive and impractical—teachers simply could not give every student the necessary time and attention. There are two answers to this. The first is that there is no alternative, education *is* personal. When it comes to expense, personalized learning is an investment, not a cost. The price of disengagement is sky high—rehabilitation programs, reengagement programs, and alternative education programs take huge amounts of budgets to sustain. The majority of them rely on personalized approaches to *re*engage young people with their education. If all education were personalized to begin with, far fewer students would *dis*engage in the first place.

The second argument is that it is possible to personalize learning for every student, especially through the creative use of new technologies. We take it for granted that most aspects of our lives *can* be personalized—from our cars to our diets to our phones—but for some reason not our education. It would be counterintuitive to be prescriptive in how to personalize learning—each school has its own unique set of circumstances, resources, and cast of characters to be taken into account. What different methods of personalized approaches to learning have in common is a passion for forming education around how individual children learn and what they need to learn to form themselves.

Personalizing education means recognizing that intelligence is diverse and multifaceted, and enabling students to pursue their particular interests and strengths. It also means adapting the schedule to the different rates at which students learn, as we will see below, and incorporating forms of assessment that support their personal progress and achievement.

Its Schedule Is Flexible

The purpose of the schedule is to facilitate learning. Rather than rotating teachers and students through the day from room to room and subject to subject, the schedule should be sensitive to the needs and requirements of each activity. If a business required that its entire workforce stop what it was doing every forty minutes to move to a different room and do something else entirely, the business would rapidly grind to a halt. When you think of it in those terms, it seems ridiculous that the majority of schools put their students and teachers through this bizarre routine. Not only is it a strange concept to expect human beings to stop what they are doing and physically move rooms at the sound of a bell, it is also counterintuitive for learning. Breaking the day up this way is another example of a school practice that makes sense from an admin point of view but little else. Different activities need more or less time than others—a group project may need several hours of uninterrupted work; a personal writing assignment may be better done in a series of shorter sessions. If the schedule is flexible and more personalized, it is more likely to facilitate the kind of dynamic curriculum that healthy ecosystems depend on for learning to happen authentically.

It Keeps Assessment in Perspective

Assessment is a controversial topic in education, but an essential part of the ecosystem. Fundamentally, assessment is the process of making judgments about students' progress and attainment, and there are two components of it: a description and an assessment. If you say that someone can swim ten lengths in a swimming pool, that is a neutral description of what they can do. If you say that they are the best swimmer in the district, that's an assessment. Assessments compare individual performances with others and rate them against particular criteria. There are several roles of assessment—diagnostic, to help teachers understand students' aptitude and levels of development; formative, to gather information on students' work and activities to support their progress; and summative, which is about making judgments on overall performance at the end of a program of work.

This all seems simple enough, but the reason assessment is a controversial topic is that it has become synonymous with standardized and high-stakes testing. Many governments and others throughout the wider education ecosystem have lost sight of the purpose of assessment. It is now used in a myriad of toxic incarnations, from international competition, to determining the outcome of a child's entire life, to whether or not a teacher will keep their job. In reality, methods of assessment can take many forms, from informal judgments in the classroom to formal assignments and public examinations. Assessment can draw on many forms of evidence, including class participation, portfolios of work, written essays, and assignments in other media. Portfolios allow for detailed descriptions of the work that students have done, with examples and reflective comments from themselves and others. In peer group assessment, students contribute to the judgments of each other's work. Great education ecosystems deploy a variety of these methods to ensure students are progressing at the appropriate rate.

The key mistake is to see assessment as the be-all and end-all of education. It is an essential part of the whole process and should interweave naturally with the daily processes of teaching and learning. It should be an integral and supportive part of the day-to-day school culture.

It Understands the Importance of Play

Play is the most natural way in which people of all ages, and particularly children, learn and make sense of the world. The importance of play has been recognized in all cultures, has been widely studied, peer reviewed, and endorsed, and yet it is far too often trivialized and even reprimanded in school environments. Importantly, as we are increasingly lowering the age that children begin school—from kindergarten to pre-K—as well as piling on structured extracurricular activities and excess homework, more and more children are missing out on this critical aspect of their development.

Children have a powerful and innate ability to learn. When left to their own devices, they explore options and make choices that we cannot and should not make for them. Play is not only a fundamental aspect of learning, but also a child's natural expression of it and a critical aspect of developing curiosity and imagination. In the case of play, the most effective action a school can take is to stand aside and let it happen. Children do not need lessons in how to play, nor do they need to be overly surveilled or scheduled—they simply require the space and freedom to do what they naturally do best.

It Makes Meaningful Connections

Great schools are continually creative in how they connect to the wider communities of which they are a part. They are not hidden away in isolation; they are hubs of learning for the whole community. Cities and other local areas have a wealth of resources and experiences for schools to engage with. Much of what children learn is cultural: they absorb the general way of life of the communities they are a part of. In engaging with local communities, everyone benefits—students have access to real-world learning opportunities, and to content and experiences that are relevant to who they are and where they live; the wider community helps to engage the next generation of active citizens.

Additionally, by connecting with families and other support systems, schools can gain a greater understanding of the students they teach. Embracing parent and caregiver participation, in particular, is a vital resource many schools either overlook or actively avoid. Many of the challenges that schools commonly face, such as bullying or discipline problems, can be spotted in the classroom but begin in the outside world. Developing closer ties with families and the community is one of the best ways to understand and tackle these issues. Healthy school ecosystems are aware of the wider ecosystems that they, and their students, fit within.

It Considers Its Physical Environment

Schools are shaped by their physical environment. You can sense the culture of a school as soon as you walk through the door. Some feel impersonal and institutional, others feel vibrant and alive. A physical environment is more than cosmetic, it affects the mood, motivation, and vitality of the whole school community.

We know much more now about the role the physical environment plays in learning than ever before. How much light is in a room, the temperature, the air quality, all play a vital role in whether an environment is conducive to learning. The furniture is important too—asking children and young people to sit on hard chairs for hours on end will naturally inhibit their ability to pay attention, yet too often they are expected to sit without wriggling or fidgeting, and certainly without complaint. Students are much more likely to be able to engage in a class if they are seated comfortably, even more so if they have a variety of options—seated, standing, at desks, on the floor, for example.

As living beings, we are dependent on sunlight and fresh air to thrive; making the most of outdoor experiences is an essential part of a thriving school environment. Different activities need different sorts of spaces and atmospheres.

It Values the Voices of Its Participants

For some reason we have systematically taken away the voices of one of our largest demographics—our children and young people. Children and young people are not impartial by-products of education, they are key to the whole operation. They are the very reason the system exists in the first place. It should not be too revolutionary a concept that they be involved in the process of deciding what happens to them, and how.

A healthy school ecosystem depends on the shared respect for individuals, empathy with the needs of the group, and the commitment of the whole community to common purposes and mutual well-being. These values should be at the heart of every school.

Creating the Conditions for Miracles

All life on Earth is miraculous. How we come to be and how we develop—that a person can go from being a tiny creature so utterly dependent on its parents for every aspect of survival to a fully grown, independent adult with a mind of their own—is miraculous. But to say it is a miracle implies that it is a rare and very occasional thing.

In human communities, as in the natural world, miracles happen every day and are essential to flourishing. As educators, our role is to create the conditions for growth, development, and learning to happen. When we get it right we discover that all along we have been in the miracle business, and it's honestly the only business to be in.

7

One Shot

Our best hope for the future is to develop a new understanding of human capacity to meet a new era of human existence.

The Dalai Lama once said that to be born at all is a miracle—and he was right. Around 100 billion people have lived and died on Earth. Take a moment to stop and think about how you actually came to be one of them. For you to have been born, all of the fine threads of your own ancestry have woven together across all the generations of humanity. How many people across those centuries had to meet each other and have lives and children until eventually your parents met? Then what happened in your parents' lives that eventually led to your birth? When you consider all the chance meetings, random introductions, circumstances, obstacles, wars, and other world-changing events—the chances of you being born at all were astronomically slim. There have been various estimates of just how slim—one has the chance of you being born at 1 in 400 trillion. Another has it at around 1 in $10^{2,685,000}$.[1] In either case, the odds were against you. Yet here you are.

You are one thread toward the bottom of an ancient and ongoing tapestry. You carry within you the biological memories of all your forebears that have influenced your ethnicity, how you look, your natural constitution, aptitudes, and personality. Of course, you are not a direct replica of your parents and ancestors, you are your own unique person crafted through a unique combination of personal characteristics that have come together in you.

We have no control over our birth—who we are born to, which genetic cocktail we inherit, and where we are born. Who we *become* is shaped by the crosscurrents of our personalities and the circumstances in which we live. Cultures are created when communities create shared ideas, values, and patterns of behavior. We are each affected by our own cultures and how they view the world. Who you become may be affected by whether you live in poverty or prosperity, in peace or war, and by your education or lack of it. Throughout your life you are presented with countless opportunities, both large and small. The ones you take and the ones you don't ultimately influence the cadence of your life. In short, from your ancestral lineage to your natural aptitudes and personality to your circumstances, your life is unique to you.

While the past may be set in stone, the future is not. This is because of our very nature as human beings and because of all that we have looked at throughout these chapters—all the multifaceted ways in which the brain works, and in particular our powers of imagination and creativity. You create your own life by how you see the world and your place in it; by the opportunities you take and the ones you refuse; by the possibilities you see and the choices you make. Life is organic; very few people can look back and say they correctly anticipated the lives they have actually led. Some may be doing roughly what they thought they might, but no one could have foreseen all of the tiny nuances: the specific job, partner, home, or children. That's because life is neither linear nor predictable. It is a constant process of improvisation between your interests and personality on the one hand and your circumstances and opportunities on the other.

Life is also finite. While you cannot predict the myriad of twists and turns your life may take, the one thing you can know with absolute certainty is that at some point it will end. It was once said that whenever you see the dates of someone's life the most important part is the dash in the middle. What did they do between birth and death?

The Crisis of Human Resources

In Western cultures we avoid death. Not the act itself, but acknowledging it—talking about it, and processing what it really means. As a result, too many people live as though it will never happen to them or the people they love. They endure their lives, get through each week, and wait for the weekend. As life goes on they increasingly feel they have lost their chance to be happy and fulfilled. We tend to believe that our capacities decline as we grow older, and that the opportunities we have missed are gone forever. We perpetuate this view in our schools, businesses, communities, and certainly in our advertising and popular culture.

The dominant Western worldview is not based on seeing synergies and connections, but on making distinctions and seeing differences. This creates sharp distinctions between the mind and the body and between human beings and the rest of nature. This may be why there is such a general lack of understanding about how the food we consume directly affects how our bodies work, and that the mass production of the goods we demand directly affects the health of the planet. The rate of self-inflicted physical illness from bad nutrition is one example of the crisis in human resources. The rates of depression, anxiety, and suicide that we discussed in chapter 2 are another. There are examples of how our systems are failing us everywhere—in the percentage of people who are not interested in the work they do, in the numbers of students who feel alienated from their education, and in the increased use of antidepressants, alcohol, and other mood-altering drugs.

On the other hand, there are people who are passionate about what they do and the lives they are living. They are connected, in tune, and fulfilled. Of course, nobody's life is completely perfect from start to finish, but these people are embracing life to the fullest. In part this is because they have discovered what it is that they truly love—they are in their Element.

Living a Life of Passion and Purpose

My books *The Element* and *Finding Your Element* dive deeply into the concept of being in our Element, but it is worth discussing some of the key points and why it is so important here. The Element is the place in which the things we love to do and the things we are good at come together. It is where natural aptitude meets personal passion. Being good at something is important, but not enough—plenty of people are good at things they don't enjoy. To be in your Element, you have to love it. There are two main features to this, and there are two conditions. The features are *aptitude* and *passion*, the conditions are *attitude* and *opportunity*. Often the process goes something like: I get it; I love it; I want it; where is it?

There are also two reasons why it is so important that each and every person discovers what this is for them. The first is personal: life is short and we only have one chance to really live it. Figuring out what you love to do is vital to understanding who you are and what you're capable of being and doing with your life. The second reason is economic: as the world evolves, the very future of our communities and institutions will depend upon our diversity of talents and aptitudes. As the world continues to change faster than ever, our best hope for the future is to develop a new paradigm of human capacity to meet a new era of human existence.

Discovering what is inside of yourself is the best guarantee of creating a rewarding life. It is also the best chance we have collectively of navigating the uncertain future that now lies before us. The Element has powerful implications for how to run our schools, businesses, communities, and institutions. The core principles of this are rooted in the wider, organic conception of human growth and development that we have looked at in the previous chapters. Systemically, we need to evolve how we nurture human talent and to understand how talent expresses itself differently in every individual.

In chapter 2 we looked at the world as it is now, as we have created it up to this point. For most of human history our ancestors could feel relatively sure of what their future would look like, and often even the future of their children and their children's children. In our times, new technologies will change the nature and course of our realities over and over again within the course of a single life span. We know this because it already has. There was a time in living history in which smartphones were inconceivable. Now it is inconceivable that we could live without them. And phones are just one example. Wi-Fi, electric cars, video calls, and social media are others—the list could go on and on. The only way to prepare for the future is to make the most of ourselves on the assumption that doing so will make us as flexible and productive as possible.

What we know for sure about the future is that it will be different, and that the rate of change today is slower than it will be tomorrow. We must therefore think very differently about human resources and about how we develop them if we are to face the future head on. It is essential that we embrace a richer conception of human capacity if we are to make the best of ourselves and of each other.

One Planet

Understanding the dynamic elements of human growth is one imperative aspect of sustaining human cultures into the future.

Understanding and protecting the ecosystems of the natural world on which we ultimately depend is another.

For far too long human beings have viewed nature as an infinite warehouse of resources and material prosperity. We have mined, logged, fished, and overrun the natural world. Through our careless behavior with the Earth's resources we have brought it gasping to its knees, and we are at a crisis point. Since the 1950s we have been in a period known as the Great Acceleration, in which the rate of impact of human activity upon the Earth's geology and ecosystems is significantly rising. Our behavior is overburdening the Earth's capacity to cater to us at a terrifying rate.

The delicate balance of life on Earth is maintained in part by a system of checks and balances. The natural world is maintained by the nuanced relationships of predators and prey. Nature has this figured out. In the Serengeti there are more than 100 prey animals to every single predator,[2] and that's because being a predator is exhausting and often unrewarding work. Other creatures have developed sophisticated techniques to avoid being dinner—such as the octopus, who can disguise itself as a jellyfish, or the frog covered in poisonous glands. None of these are foolproof plans, and so the continuous cycle of eat and be eaten endures. The problem is that we humans have successfully mitigated our risk of predators completely. Of course, in a fair fight we wouldn't stand a chance against a lion or a tiger, but we have developed ways of living that mean we now have no major predators. We have remedies for venom, sprays for insects, and have even gone so far as to eliminate predators in their own habitats should they encroach on our recreational activities—a shark who might have the audacity to swim too close to a beach, for example. The result is that we are living unchecked on this planet and we are destroying it. Unless we begin to hold ourselves accountable, both in our wider communities and as individuals, the result for us all will be catastrophic.

When we talk about saving the planet, we really mean saving our own life upon it. As we have explored, nature always finds a way for life if left to its own devices. Humans, on the other hand, are not as guaranteed a place on this planet as we seem to think. Throughout these pages we have looked at how, like all other life on Earth, we thrive in some conditions and wither in others. For the most part this has been in relation to our mental and spiritual well-being. It is just as true for our physical survival. If the planet continues to heat, if the carbon dioxide, nitrous oxide, and methane levels continue to rise, if the ocean continues to acidify—we will have succeeded in creating conditions in which human life, and much of the rest of life on Earth, cannot survive.

We are at a crisis point, but it is not yet too late. As with our own lives, the story is not yet completely written. There are actions that we can take both collectively and individually, and we must. We currently have no viable alternative to living on Earth. As far as we can tell, this planet is the only home we have, and are likely to have for a very long time.

As David Attenborough observed: "We have come as far as we have because we are the cleverest creatures to have ever lived on Earth. But if we are to continue to exist, we will require more than intelligence. We will require wisdom."

Looking Further

The crises in the worlds of nature and human resources are connected. Jonas Salk, the scientist who developed the Salk polio vaccine, reportedly made the observation that "if all the insects were to disappear from the earth, within fifty years all other forms of life would end. But if all human beings were to disappear from the earth, within fifty years all other forms of life would flourish." In other words, we have now become the problem.

Our extraordinary capacity for imagination has given rise to the most far-reaching examples of human achievement. It has literally changed the face of the planet. But it has also brought us to the brink. If we are to continue, we will need to pull on every resource of human potential we have. Up to this point we have seen far—we have looked at the Moon and we have landed on it. But we have not seen far enough. We still think too narrowly and too closely about ourselves as individuals and as a species and too little about the consequences of our actions.

To make the best of our time together on this fragile and overrun planet, our only hope is to develop our powers of imagination and creativity within a different framework of human purpose. We only have one shot.

8

Be the Change

**Rock 'n' roll was not a government-led initiative.
Revolutions do not wait for legislation;
they emerge from what people do
at the ground level.**

Who you are in this world is as much defined by what you do as what you think. It's what Eliza Doolittle meant in *My Fair Lady* when she demanded, "Don't talk of love, show me," and what Gandhi meant when he declared that "if we could change ourselves, the tendencies in the world would also change," which has often been simplified to "Be the change you wish to see in the world." You can spend your days being imaginative without achieving very much; creativity is what turns imagination into something tangible. In the same vein, you can spend your days being well intentioned without changing very much. It takes action to change the world, and it starts with you. Throughout these pages we have explored the outcome of hundreds of thousands of years of human creativity and imagination and how they have brought us here—to the crossroads of our future. In one direction, we will continue down the same road we are on, without changing our course. If we do, we will discover that we can go only so far before we come to an impasse. If we go the other direction, if we change our course, we will find a long and prosperous path that will take us to places we can hardly begin to imagine. It is essential that we choose the latter. So what will it take?

Rock 'n' Roll Was Not a Government-Led Initiative

The great revolutions in history began from the ground up. The pioneers of the American Revolution did not sit around waiting for Britain to set them free, they took action. The rebels of the French Revolution did not hope the monarchy would come to the concept of democracy on its own, they literally and figuratively set the country alight under the banner of *Liberté, Égalité, Fraternité*. Fortunately, the revolution we are calling for here requires much less bloodshed than either of these. A more recent example is of same-sex marriage, which for far too long was an unthinkable option, violently opposed by governments and religious groups alike. While the fight for LGBTQ+ rights is far from over, same-sex marriage is rightly legal in most major countries around the world, including ones with deep religious roots, such as Ireland, and strong political views, like the USA, because people rose up to demand better.

So, if revolutions are not government-led initiatives, how do they begin? One insight, attributed to Benjamin Franklin, is that there are three sorts of people in the world: those who are immovable, those who are movable, and those who move. Some people just don't see the need for change, and any attempt to reason with them falls on deaf ears. It is well enough to leave these types of people alone. They will sit like boulders in a stream, letting the waters of change run around them. Time and the tide are on the side of transformation and will leave them behind as the current moves on. Those who are movable may see the need for change, or, once it is pointed out, may wonder how they didn't see it before. In either case, they are open to learning and to acting, and once their energies are engaged they are powerful allies.

Then there are those who move: the change agents who can see the shape of a different future and are determined to bring it about through their own actions and by working with others. They don't ask for permission or wait for a starting pistol. They just move. And when enough people move, that is a movement. If the movement has enough energy, that is a revolution. Margaret Mead knew this when she said, "Never doubt that a small group of thoughtful, committed citizens can change the world; indeed, it's the only thing that ever has."

The revolution we need calls for a global reset of our social systems. It calls for a new, wider conception of human ability, and an embrace of the richness of our diversity of talents. It is based on a belief in the value of the individual, the right to self-determination, our potential to evolve, and the importance of civic responsibility and respect for others. And it begins with education.

You Are the System

If you are involved in education in any way, and when it comes down to it most of us are—whether you are a student, parent, teacher, policymaker, politician, or someone outside of the system entirely, like a business owner or other professional— what happens in schools affects you directly because it influences the generations of young people who will one day come to shape society. You have three options to create change: you can make changes within the system, you can press for changes to the system, or you can take a stand from outside the system.

Change from Within— Teachers, Principals, Policymakers

Opportunities for change exist within every school. Schools often do things simply because they've always done them that way, but many of these habits are not mandated. The best place to start thinking about how to change education is exactly where you are in it. If you are a teacher, for your students you are the system. If you are a school principal, for your community you are the system. If you are a policymaker, for the schools you control, you are the system. If you change the experiences of education for those you work with, to them you have changed the system. In doing so, you have become part of a wider, more complex process of change in education as a whole.

Education must be revolutionized from the ground up. It doesn't happen behind the closed doors of committee rooms or in the speeches of politicians. Education is what goes on between learners and teachers in actual schools. As such, there is a natural ecosystem of responsibilities in creating change:

Teachers

The role of teachers is to facilitate students' learning. If you are a teacher, you know that this is not just a job or a profession: it is a calling, and properly conceived, it is an art form. Great teachers don't just know their discipline, they know their students, and they use their expertise to respond to their students' energy and engagement. They are not only instructors, but mentors and guides who can raise the confidence of their students, help them find a sense of direction, and empower them to believe in themselves. The best way to effect daily change as a teacher is to commit to integrating these values into your daily practice.

Principals

As a principal, your role is to create the conditions in your schools in which teachers can fulfill these roles. For a school to excel, it is critical that it have an inspired school leader who brings vision and a deep understanding of the kinds of environments in which learners can and want to learn. The primary job of great principals is not to improve test results, but to build a community whose members share a common sense of purpose. Visionary principals recognize that the established conventions of schooling are secondary to these purposes.

Policymakers

The role of policymakers is to create conditions in which principals and schools can fulfill these responsibilities. Just as teachers and principals should create the conditions for growth for their own students and communities, your role is to create similar conditions for the networks of schools and communities you are appointed to serve. Culture is a set of permissions about what is and what is not acceptable behavior. As a policymaker, you can facilitate change at all levels by advocating for it—by giving schools permission to break old habits in the interests of breaking new ground.

Change from Within—
Children, Young People, Parents

There is not a simple line from vision to change. Much like the creative process, change is a constant process of action, improvisation, evaluation, and reorientation in the light of experience and circumstances. So how can you effect change if you are within the system but in a position of less control than those above?

Children and Young People

The whole education system is designed for you. It might not often feel that way, but if education is what happens between teachers and learners, you are 50 percent of that equation. More than those of any other education stakeholder, we systematically silence the voices of the young, but you are more powerful than you know. Your generation is more connected than any that has come before you. You have only ever experienced the digital age, and therefore take all these technological advancements for granted the way fish take water for granted. You are also the ones with the most at stake: if nothing changes, you will work harder for less money and higher living costs than any other generation. You will be over-qualified for the entry-level jobs you are obliged to apply for. But your generation has already begun to show us that you are passionate, determined, and taking no prisoners, from March For Our Lives to School Strike 4 Climate to the young voices of Black Lives Matter. In the case of education, it is vital that you understand your rights. Article 29 of the UN Convention on the Rights of the Child states that education shall be directed to "the development of the child's personality, talents and mental and physical abilities to their fullest potential." Don't settle for anything less.

Parents

In 2018 we published *You, Your Child, and School*. This was in response to the overwhelming number of messages we received from parents who were concerned about the education their children were receiving, and who wanted to know what they could do. There is a lot parents can do. Teaching and learning is a relationship, and one of the most important parts of it is between you and the school. Your children are more likely to do well at school if you avoid thinking of school and teachers having sole responsibility for their education. You can begin by building a healthy relationship with your child's teachers. This does not mean questioning their every judgment or decision, it means being their ally. Teachers see parts of your child in certain circumstances, but they don't have access to the whole picture. You can help illuminate the aspects they are in the dark about, and vice versa. You can also join a parent-teacher association and become actively involved in the culture of the school. You can take this a step further and join the school board. You can petition for change. How you choose to get involved is dependent on your personal circumstances. It is not realistic to expect that every parent has the time and resources to dedicate to fully embedding themselves within the school community, and it may be that for your family these aren't the best options. When it comes to your child, the very best you can do in this context is to help them develop in their unique ways and create opportunities for them to identify the personal talents and interests that engage them the most. Fundamentally, you are your child's best advocate: do not trust the system more than you trust your own child, and do not trust the system more than you trust your instincts as a parent.

Changing from the Outside

There are many people who work in other professions who can work alongside teachers and bring their energy, enthusiasm, and specific expertise to education. Bringing the real world into the classroom is an essential part of helping students discover new paths and options they may otherwise not know exist. Even if you are not directly involved in education on a daily basis, your voice is still a critical component of the revolution. So what can you do as a business or an individual?

Businesses

All organizations are competing in a world in which the ability to innovate and adapt to change is a necessity to stay ahead. When they become stuck in old habits, they risk missing the wave of change that will carry more innovative companies forward. All organizations are perishable—they are created by people and need to be constantly revitalized if they are to survive. In order to flex and adapt, a business must create conditions in which each and every person involved in it is connected to their creative capacities. It is a critical error to see some roles as creative and others as not. Being a creative leader involves strategic roles in three areas: facilitating the creative abilities of every member of the organization; firming and facilitating dynamic creative teams; and promoting a general culture of innovation. This all becomes easier if you are not starting from the beginning, if the people you are hiring have already had opportunities to connect with themselves holistically throughout their educations. As well as creating a culture within your business, making strong connections with schools and other organizations is an important part of the ecosystem. You can do this by creating opportunities for learning in the real world through paid internships. In the past, internships have been used by many businesses as opportunities to have menial or undesirable tasks completed for free. The real purpose of internships is to provide opportunities for young people to explore different career paths and gain experience in real settings. For your business, the benefit of providing internship opportunities is not only to spot new talent, and to benefit from the energy of young people; it is also to play your part in raising and nurturing the generation you will one day come to hire, and who in turn will become a pivotal part of making your company a success.

Internships are not just for young people. The era of a single lifelong career is in the past, and as such you would be wise to create opportunities for people at all stages of life to experience your company and culture. The most important part of an internship program is to ensure it is paid—very few people can dedicate their time and energy in a professional capacity for free. By only offering unpaid internships, you narrow the pool of applicants to those who can afford it. The more people who have a fair shot, the more impactful the whole process becomes.

Individuals

If none of the above categories have felt applicable to you, there are several ways you can become involved in the revolution. One way is to add your voice, to share resources and spread the message.

We receive countless messages from people who are desperately relieved to have finally discovered that all along the problem hasn't been with them or their children, the problem has been with the system. By sharing the core messages we have outlined here, you are providing lifelines. Another is to dedicate the time and energy required to discover your Element, if you don't already know what it is. We have discussed how essential it is that we embrace a richer conception of human intelligence, that we celebrate the diversity of talent that makes our species so unique, and that each and every person discover what it is that they truly love to do—that means you. Once you have discovered this, or if you already know, you can become a mentor. Mentors serve an invaluable role in helping people identify their passions, encouraging their interests, and pushing them to make the most of their capacities. Without mentors, the journey is considerably harder. The most valuable thing you can do is to commit to living a life of passion and purpose yourself, and encourage others to do the same.

Collectively Changing Our Habits

The revolution we need requires advocating for fundamental shifts in the ways in which our societies function. It calls for waking up to the culture of toxic behaviors we have come to take for granted and acting more intentionally as a result. If we are to achieve this, we can no longer take a passive stance when it comes to the future of our planet.

There are many resources dedicated to the changes we must make if we are to stop global warming, and almost all of them advocate for the same actions: we must significantly reduce our greenhouse gas emissions, end our overuse of fertilizers, stop decimating land for farming and oceans for fishing, replace fossil fuels with cleaner energy, and we must change the way we eat and consume. Of all of these, the one within the control of every individual is to change the way they eat—to consume less fish and animal products. It is also the most contentious issue.

It is striking how many people say, "I would watch that film or read that book, but I know that when I do I will have to change my habits and I'm not sure I want to." It's true that the only thing necessary for the triumph of evil is for good men to do nothing. It is no longer an option to stick our heads in the sand. If we were to choose less meat, we would free up farmland for rewilding and the growth of crops that have a smaller impact on the environment. If we were to choose less fish, we could set large portions of the oceans aside as no-take zones.

It is not practical for every culture in the world to stop eating meat or fish completely—they are ingrained in their cultural and religious traditions. For some communities, they are staples of their diets and economy. But for those of us who live in metropolitan areas and have a wide variety of choice, committing to choosing alternatives means doing our part in finding a sustainable balance.

If we are to create a better future for ourselves and for our children, we must take proactive steps in protecting the conditions on Earth that will sustain us to do so.

Be the Change

The world is undergoing revolutionary changes. Like most revolutions, the one we are calling for has been brewing for a long time and is gathering pace. We know what works in education; there are examples of schools and programs around the world that do these things every day. Effective education is always a balance between tradition and innovation, rigor and freedom, the individual and the group, the inner world and the outer world. As we swing between the two poles the task is to help find an equilibrium, and the need is urgent. Revolutions are not only defined by the ideas that drive them but by the scale of their impact. The ideas behind this revolution have been around for a long time, but there is an increasing shift in energy—the revolution is well under way. We create the worlds in which we live, and we can re-create them. It takes courage and imagination, and we have plenty of both in store.

Imagine If . . .

"The lesson we most need to learn is that there is more to life on Earth than human beings and more to being human than self-interest. Our futures all depend on learning this lesson by heart." 1

—Sir Ken Robinson, 2018

Of all the abilities we humans are equipped with, we undervalue our imagination the most. We view it as something infantile that needs to be grown out of as soon as possible, or, if not completely eradicated, at least kept under control. We use it to criticize or undermine by telling people they have an "overactive imagination." We pride ourselves on being "down-to-earth" and "in touch with reality," as if a lack of imagination is a sign of being trustworthy and reliable. And yet the great tragedy is that in addition to being what separates us from the rest of life on Earth, our incredible capacity for imagination is what has made our lives, as they are now, possible. Imagination led us out of caves and into cities and replaced superstition with science. It is fundamental in every aspect of your life, from the seat you are sitting on to the pen on your desk to the music you love. Indoor plumbing, central heating, and modern medicine are all examples of imagination advancing the human experience, as were Beethoven's Fifth, Frida Kahlo's *Watermelons*, Kenneth MacMillan's *Manon*, and Kobe Bryant's fadeaway.

All of our great advancements have been sparked by one simple phrase: "Imagine if . . ." Two words, endless possibilities. Within this simple phrase, ideas have been ignited and worlds have been changed. Imagination in this form requires questioning what currently exists and designing an alternative. It is how human cultures progress. It is also how they fall. From the fall of Rome to the decline of the British Empire, history has shown us time and time again that no civilization, business, or individual is indestructible. Throughout our history, imagination has taken us to wondrous heights and devastating lows. To navigate the turbulent times we are experiencing, it is our only hope. The challenges we face are significant and complex; to solve them we have to become more creative, not less. The climate crisis is the result of our disengagement from the natural world. To solve it, we have to become more engaged, not less. To tackle the existential problems in our cultures, we have to become more human, not less.

The beauty of the phrase "Imagine if . . ." is that it is open-ended. It is provocative rather than prescriptive, and endlessly adaptable. Imagine if . . . we could control fire. Imagine if . . . you could fly from one side of the world to the other. Imagine if . . . we could land on the Moon. Imagine if . . . two people could marry regardless of gender. Imagine if . . . we valued dance as much as mathematics. Imagine if . . . we had a cure for terminal cancer. Imagine if . . . we re-created the systems we take for granted so they encouraged every single person to thrive. Imagine if . . .

It is impossible for any one person to solve every problem in the world. The problems we face are too numerous, too complicated, and too stubborn for one person alone. And yet without the dedicated actions of passionate and compassionate individuals, our shared obstacles would never be overcome. Any movement begins with individuals, and when they come together, the world changes. As Ursula K. Le Guin so powerfully said: "Any human power can be resisted and changed by human beings."

The changes we urgently need are rooted in every individual's right to live an evolved and fulfilled life, and in the importance of cultivating civic responsibility and respect for others. They are about promoting human dignity, equity, and fairness. They are essential to improving the quality of people's lives today and to manifesting the world we hope to live in tomorrow. These principles have always mattered, but the need for change is more critical now than ever. This is not only about the lives of individuals: It's about the character of our civilizations. It's about creating a future for us all.

Notes

Chapter 2: The World We Have Created

1. It's worth recalling how quickly this has happened. The iPhone and its imitations became available only in 2007, the iPad in 2010. People everywhere scrambled to get them.
2. https://www.who.int/teams/mental-health-and-substance-use/suicide-data.
3. https://www.mhe-sme.org/young-people-and-mental-health-infographic/.
4. Stein Emil Vollset et al., "Fertility, Migration, and Population Scenarios for 195 Countries and Territories from 2017 to 2100: A Forecasting Analysis for the Global Burden of Disease Study," *The Lancet* 396, no. 10258 (2020): 1285–1306, https://www.thelancet.com/journals/lancet/article/PIIS0140-6736(20)30677-2/fulltext.

Chapter 5: From the Factory to the Farm

1. Timothy F. Landers et al., "A Review of Antibiotic Use in Food Animals: Perspective, Policy, and Potential," *Public Health Reports* 127 (January–February 2012): 4–22, https://www.ncbi.nlm.nih.gov/pmc/articles/PMC3234384/pdf/phr12700004.pdf.
2. Christian Lindmeier, "Stop Using Antibiotics in Healthy Animals to Prevent the Spread of Antibiotic Resistance," World Health Organization, November 7, 2017, https://www.who.int/news/item/07-11-2017-stop-using-antibiotics-in-healthy-animals-to-prevent-the-spread-of-antibiotic-resistance.
3. Antibiotic resistance happens naturally, but the misuse of antibiotics in both humans and animals is expediting the process. Antibiotic resistance

is rising to dangerously high levels in all parts of the world. World Health Organization fact sheet, "Antibiotic Resistance," WHO, July 31, 2020, https://www.who.int/news-room/fact-sheets/detail/antibiotic-resistance.

4. A 2005 study by Chapin et al. found that 98 percent of bacteria in air samples isolated from an indoor swine feeding-operation were resistant to at least two antibiotics commonly used in swine production. Amy Chapin et al., "Airborne Multidrug-Resistant Bacteria Isolated from a Concentrated Swine Feeding Operation," *Environmental Health Perspectives* 113, no. 2 (2005): 137–42, https://ehp.niehs.nih.gov/doi/pdf/10.1289/ehp.7473. A 2008 study by Graham et al. (https://journals.sage-pub.com/doi/pdf/10.1177/003335491212700103) tested air and surface samples collected behind vehicles transporting poultry and found them to contain significantly more antibiotic-resistant bacteria than those collected behind control vehicles.

5. Jeff McMahon, "Why Agriculture's Greenhouse Gas Emissions Are Almost Always Underestimated," *Forbes*, December 2, 2019, https://www.forbes.com/sites/jeffmcmahon/2019/12/02/5-reasons-agricultures-greenhouse-gas-emissions-are-usually-underestimated/?sh=1f1c1d4e6ac8.

6. World Health Organization fact sheet, "Adolescent Mental Health," WHO, September 28, 2020, https://www.who.int/news-room/fact-sheets/detail/adolescent-mental-health.

Chapter 7: One Shot

1. Mel Robbins, "How to Stop Screwing Yourself Over," TEDx San Francisco, June 2011, www.ted.com/talks/mel_robbins_how_to_stop_screwing_yourself_over/transcript? language=en, and Dina Spector, "The Odds of You Being Alive Are Incredibly Small," *Insider*, June 11, 2012, www.businessinsider.com/infographic-the-odds-of-being-alive-2012-6.

2. David Attenborough, *A Life on Our Planet*, 2020.

Imagine If...

1. Sir Ken Robinson, from his contribution to *Genius: 100 Visions of the Future*, published in 2018 by the Genius 100 Foundation.